THE HERETIC'S TAROT

THE HERETIC'S TAROT

By

Boniface Wolfsong

First Edition

The Lycian Sanctuary
San Antonio, Texas

The Heretic's Tarot

The Lycian Sanctuary
San Antonio, Texas
USA

Table of Contents

Table of Contents

The Heretic's Tarot

Preface

Over the years, I have started and stopped writing this book so many times, that I have lost track of the number. Each time I would begin to write, I would discover some new line of research, or talk to friends about the ideas in it and then, because of these discussions, start whole new lines of thought relating to the subject of the Tarot. I have always asked for honest straightforward opinions about my theories on the Tarot, especially with any that seemed shaky or misinformed. It was always my closest friends that asked the most difficult questions and tested the "secret layout" the best. Much of this book would not have been possible, if it had not been for these friends.

First, I want to thank my best friend and confidant, my wife Elizabeth, or as others know her, Seshen. She has helped me in so many ways, too numerous to even count. She and I have discussed everything related to this subject and everything else in between. My talks with her are one of my favorite activities and I look forward to many more in our future, as we grow old together. I love you, my dear wife.

I want to thank my daughters Catherine and Alexandria for their support and questions through the years. I have "bounced" many ideas off their little heads, which are no longer so little, and gotten many needed opinions, from a younger audience, through them.

I would also like to thank the members of the first "Circle" I belonged to. We called ourselves "the Knights of the Sword and Chalice" and were together for nine years. We did a few magical rituals, but more often than not, we talked; we talked philosophy, mythology, ceremonial magic, and religion. It was through these discussions that the final form of the "Lycian Wheel of the Year" came into being and began a part of the process of finding the "secret layout" of the Tarot. Thank you David, Cynthia and Bobby.

Thanks also to the members of Wolfsong Coven, with a special thanks to two of its members who gave me the most difficult time "getting things right," Bria and Dodie. Thanks my friends, for all the questions and for putting me through my paces.

I also want to thank the Unlimited Thought Bookstore in San Antonio, Texas. It was because of their generous contribution of a meeting room, for so many years, that allowed me to hold workshops on Wicca and the Tarot. It was through these workshops I was able to present the "secret layout" to many people in the area and get a "feel" for how the general public would accept it, and where they had problems with it. I appreciate the help from the bookstore, and all who attended the workshops during those years.

Two of the people I have thanked above, have now "crossed the veil," David and Bria. I know the two of you are on to new adventures and new lives. Good luck in all you do, my friends, my love goes with you.

Introduction

This book is about a system that underlies the structure of the Tarot cards; a system that hid a heresy and a means of passing the teachings of that heresy on to others by using the cards as an instructional device. The system, or pattern, hidden in the Tarot has been spoken of, in rumor, since the cards first made their appearance in Europe, so long ago. Tarot author Richard Roberts says, "According to legends, if the twenty-two cards of the Tarot Major Arcana are placed in the correct arrangement so that they can be 'read' meaningfully not only horizontally but also vertically, then their relation to one another will be apparent, and their deepest esoteric meanings will be revealed.[1]" Some have tried to elaborate on what they believed to be the system of the Tarot by linking it with other systems which were better known, and so, easier to expound upon. One of these other systems was the Kabbala. This, however, still did not bring out into the open the original system

---

1 *Campbell, Joseph, and Richard Roberts. Tarot Revelations. 3rd ed. Vernal Equinox Press, 1987. Back cover.*

inherent in the "secret layout" of the deck and to this day there still remains much disagreement as to how the various parts of the Kabbala and its "Tree of Life" glyph line up with the cards of the Tarot.

It is said that the real secret of the Tarot is hidden in the form of the figure in the classic Hanged Man card. I have discovered this to be true. The "correct arrangement" of the cards, that reveals their meaning, is connected to the "Hanged Man" figure. I will reveal my reasoning for this connection during the course of this book and explain it fully in the final chapter.

This book is also about a theological method of interpreting the Tarot cards that is today used in the Lycian Tradition of the Craft, but can be used by other traditions as well, including those not related to Wicca at all. It makes use of a strictly Pagan system of symbols, to understand the relationship of the cards one to another. Because this system is derived from the cards themselves, in their classical renditions, rather than a later imposed foreign system, it may be the closest we can get to the original intentions and meanings the creators of the cards first gave them. Of course, how close is something we will probably never know for sure. Nonetheless, by using this method, the deck can become a very useful tool for Pagan religious instruction and can even help the most experienced members of the Craft gain new insights into our religion and its practices. The Tarot may even become that "missing" holy book which is so apparently absent in the Wiccan religion. Some may point to the "Book of Shadows," that Wiccans use as that holy book, but it does not fulfill the function of "Holy Book" as each Book of Shadows is different from one to another and do not bridge the traditions of the religion as the Tarot is capable of doing.

Many will be curious how I came to discover this "secret layout" when so many others have failed to find it; that is understandable. As I explain the pattern and how I came to know it, it will become clear there was nothing extremely difficult about any single step taken to discover it. The revelation of the "secret layout" simply relies on common sense and Ockham's Razor that states, "all things being equal, the least complicated explanation is usually the right one." I also had another thing going in my favor; luck. The fact that a long series of simple deductions were necessary to reveal the Tarot's secret does not make the overall system a simple one; looked at in its entirety, it has layer upon layer of meaning and is quite complex. This is as it should be, for any great system of teaching should be capable of bestowing meaning to a wide range of people with different backgrounds, experiences, and education. This is what the Tarot does in this "secret spread" and I am sure, once I have explained its system, others will derive even more meaning from it than I have been capable of doing. What I also found, was the "secret spread" does not relate to just the "Major Arcana," which are the Trump cards, but makes use of every card in the Tarot deck.

Let me say right from the beginning that I have absolutely no "proof" that this is "the" system or pattern the originators of the Tarot had in mind when they developed it. We do not even know if it was developed in a conscious manner, or if the pattern came about in a more natural way from the subconscious group mind, much as a dream, or myth, is created. What I know is that, in the years of my teaching this system, privately, in covens, and in public workshops, no one ever said it did not make perfect sense to them. Many also said, it opened up the Tarot in a way that allowed them to interpret the cards more easily and to meditate on them for spiritual insight as well. So, even though there is no verifiable "proof" that this is "the" rumored secret spread that reveals the hidden meaning of the Tarot, it certainly appeals to common sense and can be used without having to impose a foreign system on the cards. The only proof available for this system will be your own common sense and reason. Whether or not you accept the spread in this book, as creating a coherent picture of the Pagan cosmology of the Tarot, is entirely your decision to make.

THE HERETIC'S TAROT

The Heretic's Tarot

The Tarot as a Teaching Tool

How was the Tarot deck used in the past to teach? I became acutely aware of how it may have been done because of one particular event that happened to me as a teacher of the Wiccan Craft. I am very public as a priest of the Craft and, from time to time, someone will come to me and ask if I can give them some information about, or even teach them, the Craft. Normally, I recommend a basic book, and if they are still interested after having read that book, then we discuss the details of learning the Craft.

This one particular time, an acquaintance of mine from work asked if I could teach him about the Craft. I, unfortunately, fell into my old habit of telling him about a good basic book that would tell him more then I could at the time, and allow him to develop some questions, which I would then willingly try to answer later. Having given him the book, some days later, I asked him how it was going. He told me he had not had a chance to get to it yet. Two weeks later, I again asked him about the book and he gave me the same response. About a month

1

after I had originally given him the book, he returned it to me and appeared very embarrassed. He told me that he had never learned how to read and could not use the book, so he was returning it. I offered to teach him the Craft orally, but he told me he did not wish to take the time that doing that would involve. I was stumped. The fellow couldn't read and I felt he thought it was an imposition to ask me to teach him orally. Because he hadn't read the book, he had not developed any questions that we could sit down and discuss. So, I let the subject drop. That was my mistake, as he obviously was interested enough in the Craft to have asked about it in the first place.

Some time after this incident, I tried to think of alternatives to what I had done. I began to think about how the ancient members of a heretical belief system, at a time when the majority of the people were illiterate, would have taught one another. Then it hit me. I am a Freemason and had experience with Masonic ritual and the fraternity's use of "trestle boards" for instruction. The trestle boards are like large posters with various Masonic symbols placed on them. Each trestle board is without words and the symbols grouped on any particular board are related to one Degree, which is a ritual initiation, and the lessons associated with it.

Examples of "trestle boards" used in Freemasonry.

These trestle boards are what had first got me curious about Freemasonry. I had originally bought a book titled "Lightfoot's Manual of the Lodge[2]" and it had several trestle boards in it as illustrations. I wondered about them and figured I would read the book to find out what

2 *Lightfoot, Jewel P. Lightfoot's Manual of the Lodge. Masonic Home and School, Fort Worth, Texas. 1934.*

they meant. I discovered, though, that the book did not explain what the trestle boards meant. These illustrations were simply intended to remind a brother Mason of the secret portions of the ritual they had already experienced in the lodge. So, here was a set of pictures that had purposely been created to act as "visual notes" about a secret ritual or teaching, intelligible only to those that had already been initiated into the fraternity, and yet, they made me very curious as to their meaning. I developed many questions and became so curious about what the answers could possibly be, that I eventually joined the fraternity.

I also began to think of those paintings and drawings associated with alchemy, the ones that are so mysterious and whose meanings have been the subject of so much debate. Here was another set of "boards" with clusters of symbols on them. What suddenly occurred me was that Wicca also had its own set of "trestle boards," or at least, the Paganism of old Western Europe did. These boards, or rather illustrations with symbols on them, were the cards of the Tarot.

Here were the pictorial "notes" I needed to communicate with my illiterate friend and get him curious again about the Wiccan Craft, just as I had become interested in Freemasonry by means of the trestle boards I saw in that book.

I had been a reader and teacher of the Tarot for many years and had often related them to the fundamentals of the Wiccan Craft. What I should have done with my friend was to immediately offer him a Tarot deck. If he had taken a deck with him, after having returned that book, he would not have had any feelings of inadequacy, because the language of the Tarot is a purely pictorial one. He would have looked at the cards and maybe tried to figure out what the pictures meant, as I had done with the Masonic trestle boards, and with time, he might have understood some of the symbolism. More importantly, it would have piqued his curiosity and may have provoked questions about those symbols on the cards and why they are used in relation to one another in the particular way the Tarot uses them. Returning to me to ask those questions would have given me the opportunity to tell him about the Craft by means of the Tarot deck, and it would have given him a visual memory aid in learning the Craft. The first step, though, should have been handing him a Tarot deck and allow him the time to look at the cards, and I should have done this as soon as I found out he could not read. Now that's a lot of should-haves. I did not think of this idea in time though, because we parted company before the idea occurred to me.

That was a missed opportunity. I resolved not let such an occurrence happen again. I began to study the Tarot with two goals in mind: first, being able to teach Pagan thought by means of its symbols, and second, discovering the rumored "secret spread" in the deck that would reveal the teachings hidden within it, by its originators. This would be different from the normal use of the cards as a divinatory tool, as I would not go into the cards' use in this way, but instead, only try to discover how they could reflect the heretical teachings of an ancient Pagan belief system. I had been studying the cards for quite some years and had read about the rumors that there was an underlying system to the cards which tell of a time when the old Pagan ways had to be hidden from the religious authorities in power. I also felt that learning about the Craft in this manner would be of interest to many people, even if they have no problem with reading, as my friend did. This book is the result of my studies in the Wiccan Craft, the Masonic Craft, alchemy, ceremonial magic, Kabbala and the Tarot.

Wicca has many different Traditions within it and many different ways of practicing the religion. The Tarot is a book with many pages, many illustrations, and few or no words. In fact, the older forms of the Tarot did not even have the titles of the cards on them anywhere. This is because the figures on the cards were easily recognizable to anyone of that period, since they were simply illustrations of the people and events that populated their own environment.

By using the Tarot as a "holy book" or at least as a "book of instruction" for the Wiccan Craft, maybe we can not only learn more, but also find common ground upon which the different

Traditions can meet. Because the Tarot cards are subject to interpretation, I think that they are the perfect vehicle for this purpose. They open themselves up to various teachings, that make up the different traditions of the Craft today.

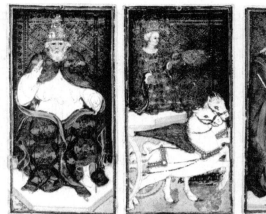

The Oldest Tarot cards known had no titles or numbers on them.

The Secret Layout of the Tarot

I will now briefly described the "secret layout" of the cards, so that you get an overall picture of where we are headed as I explain how it was discovered. I will not go into any of the specific details of the layout here, but leave that for later.

First, the deck is divided into three "levels;" the upper, middle, and lower. A portion of the deck represents each level. Think of a round cake with three separate layers. The upper layer of the cake is the realm of the deities; the Trump cards represent those deities. The middle layer is the realm of human action and human beings; these are represented by the "Court Cards," which are the kings, queens, knights and knaves. The lowest layer represents the "Pip" cards; these represent the primal creative forces of Nature.

Now, we are going to cut the cake into four equal pieces. Each piece will still have all three layers within it. Each piece represents one quarter of the entire circle of the cake and each of the four suits in the Tarot. The whole cake represents our cosmos. In the top layer of each piece of cake are five Trump cards, totaling twenty deity cards for all four pieces. I will explain where the last two Trump cards fit, in just a bit. In the middle layer of each piece of cake are four Court cards, totaling sixteen. In the lowest layer of each piece are ten Pip cards, totaling forty.

The last two cards to be placed are the Fool and Mage. The Fool card is represented by the outer frosting and the frosting between the layers of the cake, which is symbolic of the spiraling journey he makes to the center where the Mage card is located, at the intersection of the four pieces of cake. In this pattern, each card has a very specific place and meaning; these details will be explained later.

For now, you have a general idea of what the secret layout looks like in three dimensions. Here is the pattern laid out flat with the top layer being the outer ring of pentagrams, represented by human figures with arms and legs extended, the middle layer court cards being the next inward ring of equal armed crosses and the lowest layer pips being the innermost ring of tetractyses. The Fool card wanders the outer perimeter while the Magician card stands at the center of the circle, which I call the "crossroads" where the four quarters meet. The 78 dots represent the individual cards themselves.

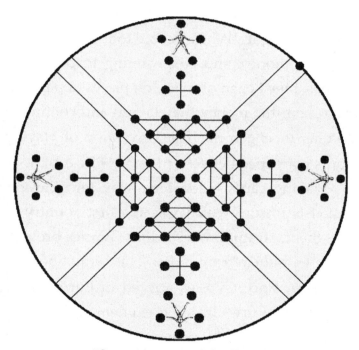

"Secret Layout of the Tarot"

Historical Environment Surrounding the Tarot's Origins

I will now explain how I arrived at this secret layout and what it all means. But first, a little history.

Playing cards were first invented in China. The Chinese government had invented paper money, and common people created gambling games using it. When people found themselves without money, and still wanting to play their games, they began drawing on pieces of paper to represent the money they lacked and continued to play their games. This invention of playing cards happened between 618 and 908 c.e.[3]

Playing cards made their way into Europe, but it is unsure which was the first country to use them. Tradition has it that Gypsies brought them with them from India. This cannot be true, however, since Gypsies arrived in Europe after card gaming was already documented there. We do know that card games were being played well before the addition of the trump cards,

---

3 *Hargrave, Catherine Perry. A History of Playing Cards. Houghton Mifflin Co., Boston, 1930. P. 6.*

which made the cards into the traditional Tarot deck of seventy-eight.

The Inquisition was established in Toulouse, France in November 1229, and the process of ridding the area of the Cathar heresy began. Under Pope Gregory IX the Inquisition was given enormous power to suppress the heresy. A campaign was started in 1233, burning vehement and relapsed Cathars wherever they were found. The Cathar heresy was of great interest to the church and its members were forcibly being converted or killed. Later in the early 1300s, a flurry of activity, especially pertaining to religion and spiritual beliefs, began taking place. The Knights Templar, as an organization, was destroyed on Friday, October 13, 1307. Many of the knights escaped capture and it was these knights that were now part of a growing underground with an agenda in conflict with that of the Catholic Church. Evidence has since become known, that some of the Templars became a part of the Masonic Fraternity and could well have influenced its rituals and teachings. The Renaissance was just beginning.

Because of a new interest in science and the myths of ancient Paganism, notions long held sacrosanct by the church and those in authority were beginning to be questioned. The Inquisition was now in full swing during this time and the pope had approved the use of torture, so hiding anything that even hinted of heresy was very necessary to avoid the attention of those with this papal authority. It was in this spiritual atmosphere that the Tarot first made its appearance.

First Appearances of the Tarot in Western Europe

It is not known where, or exactly when, the Tarot first came into being. What is known is when the deck first started to make its appearance in Western Europe, and about the attitude, of those in positions of power, toward those things that the Tarot cards seemed to deal with. It was in 1332 that Alfonse XI, King of Leon and Castile set the first documented ban against playing cards.[4] The cards must have been fairly evolved by that point or a game

---

4 Butler, Bill. *Dictionary of the Tarot. Schocken Books, New York, 1975. P. 3.*

would not have been possible. "Although the Tarot has come down to us as part of a card game it does not predate the ordinary playing card pack. The Tarot is characterized by the twenty-two cards that we nowadays call Trump cards, although they were originally called trionfi or Triumphs. Trionfi are first mentioned in 1422 and the term tarrochi from which the word Tarot derives does not appear until 1516.[5]" The environment of the time was one of suspicion, due mainly to the inquisition and the attitudes that it fostered in the people themselves, especially about things unknown or mysterious. Christianity was relatively new to the area and the older Pagan practices were slowly either being eradicated or assimilated by the church.

The art of the period indicates a need by artisans to represent the older, more traditional beliefs in their work, or even, their displeasure with the Catholic Church. Remnants of this can be seen in the old Christian churches, which

---

5 Knight, Gareth. *The Treasure House of Images*. *Destiny Books, Rochester, Vermont, 1986. P. 11.*

included in their structures Pagan iconography, placed there by the masons who built them. Paintings of the time stressed either Christian religious themes or those of the classical Pagan myths. At times, satire and criticism against the church by the builders, maybe members of the old Pagan belief system, was placed into the churches themselves. For example: "In the St. Sebaldus Church, Nuremburg, is a carving in stone showing a nun in the embrace of a monk. In Strasbourg, a hog and a goat may be seen carrying a sleeping fox as a sacred relic, in advance a bear with a cross and a wolf with a taper. An ass is reading mass at an altar.... In the Cathedral of Brandenburg a fox in priestly robes is preaching to a flock of geese; and in the Minster at Berne the Pope is placed among those who are lost in perdition.[6]" The pagan symbolism itself, though, was not receiving the main focus of these works. What the builders were doing was hiding their religious opinions and symbols in such a way that others of like

---

6 *Newton, Joseph Fort. The Builders: A Story and Study of Masonry. Plain Label Books, 1924. P. 107.*

mind could discern their meaning and yet still remain hidden from those in power who would persecute them.

There was a hidden undercurrent of pagan belief and practice very late after Christianity first started to gain its influence on the monarchs of the Western Europe. Examples of this undercurrent are evident in Alchemy, Rosicrucianism, Freemasonry and Hermeticism. Each of these systems hides a set of practices, which involved a tolerance for those beliefs, not one's own. Because the regular pack of playing cards predated the trump cards of the Tarot, it is quite possible and likely that they were added to the other cards as an afterthought, but not one without meaning. The intention may well have been to do what was being done in these other fields of interest and hide something of the old pagan faith in the cards. "The Visconti-Sforza cards are typical of a number of sumptuously produced hand-painted and gilded sets that would hardly seem suited for actual playing at cards, even by the most opulent of princes. If they were objets d'art for display, and it seems that they may have been subjects for meditation, or instruction, as magical images by those who were in the know. Even the Popes were interested in magic in those days -- sometimes quite enthusiastically.[7]" This was something, which was not held to be an admirable quality in the Christian church. The Church's official stance was that the true and only way to know the divine was the Christian way and all others were to be condemned or eradicated. Therefore, these systems had to devise methods for hiding the true meaning of their teachings. The Alchemists used the symbolism of the chemical laboratory to communicate their meaning. The Freemasons used the implements of the building trade to do the same thing. Those "in the know" would never have expected to become a Freemason and learn how to build an actual structure, or become an Alchemist and literally achieve the physical experiments of which they spoke. They used allegories and metaphor to communicate spiritual truths in an environment

---

7 Knight, Gareth. *The Treasure House of Images. Destiny Books, Rochester, Vermont, 1986. P. 13.*

that was not favorable to open dialogue about religious beliefs. The reproductions of the Visconti cards show signs of their having been "thumbtacked" to a wall for display. If an individual was studying or meditating on the cards, simply laying them on a table would have been sufficient, but the cards were tacked to a wall, which would allow a number of people in a room to view them at the same time. Doing this would have allowed an instructor to teach from the cards to a groups of students, much like modern-day Freemasons teach from their trestle boards.

There were points of overlap between the two divergent practices of Christianity and Paganism. One of these was the very real belief that there were four elements, which combined to make all those things, which existed in the world. The four elements, although not a principle teaching of Christianity, were considered to be of a secular nature and therefore not impinging on the domain of religious instruction, which the church reserved for itself. It was these four elements that opened a door of opportunity for the heretical creators of the Tarot to say something about their beliefs, that were in direct conflict with the Christian doctrine, and yet keep it hidden through symbols.

I would like to say something about the nature of these four elements. Today, we know that the elements are many more than four and the periodic table lists them very well. Many people today laugh at the ancients because they believed that there were only four elements in their conceptualization of the world. I believe we should not be so quick to judge. In reading the ancient sources, it becomes very apparent that what the ancients were speaking of was not "the elements" as we know them today. What they were referring to was "states of matter" and guess what? We, even today in our modern world, have only four states of matter. These four states are: solid, liquid, gas and plasma. These four states of matter related to what the ancients called "the elements" in this manner: earth to solid, water to liquid, air to gas and fire to plasma. So, when you hear of the "ancient elements" you should automatically be thinking "states of matter."

The four elements were the jumping off point for the creators of the Tarot to say something, which was not "technically" crossing the boundary, which the church had drawn, into heresy. It is upon these four elements, represented by the suits, that the structure of the Tarot deck is based. The suits are four in number and they have associations with the four elements, from which it was believed all that existed was composed of, through a variety of combinations. In the *Turba Philosophorum*, the oldest extant treatise in the Latin language on Alchemy, the Sixth Dictum states, "You speak only about four natures; and each one of you observes something concerning these. Now, I testify unto you that all things which God hath created are from these four natures, and the things which have been created out of them return into them. In these living creatures are generated and die, and all things take place as God hath predestinated." These four elements and their combinations also influenced the entire structure of the Tarot, as we shall see.

Because of the need to keep the actual "heretical" teachings hidden, those ancient teachers had to devise a way of passing their knowledge on without giving themselves away too blatantly. The method used was analogy and symbolism. There were key phrases taught to all students, which would give them a clue how to go on to learn this material. Those phrases included such sayings as "Like produces like," "As above, so below," and others which pointed beyond the superficial meanings given to their teachings. Often the words "Of the Wise" were used to refer to a difference between a common object and that same object, being called "of the wise," being used as a symbol for something of a more spiritual nature. For example, there was gold and everyone wants gold, true enough. Then there is the "gold of the wise," which is better than common gold. This gold was symbolic for riches beyond the ordinary material gains possible in this life. These riches referred to the riches of the spirit. Gold, the metal with which we are familiar is pointing to something like gold and yet is not gold. This was the way these teachers found to communicate their wisdom. Common, everyday things could be taken as symbols of spiritual concepts and spoken of openly. Ordinary folk would think the subject of these discourses to be the common thing spoken of, but those with the "keys" knew better. What were those keys? The meanings of the symbols themselves, usually given to those who had gone through some sort of initiation or training and having taken an oath of secrecy, this to protect them from the Inquisition. This method of using symbols was a hallmark of the Pythagorean schools, that couched their teachings in such language that the average person thought there was nothing of interest being said and yet, when explained, revealed the most profound wisdom.

The thing about using symbols to communicate is that after one knows the meaning of a few symbols, those symbols can be combined to derive or impart even more information. The Tarot cards do just that. In the

Tarot, we find many symbols, all in pictorial form, and they are represented in combination with other symbols to say something to the viewer. What exactly was being said, though, was not apparent to anyone not having the keys, or the "true meanings," of the symbols in a pagan context. The cards were just used in playing the games that were fun, but they contained the essence of pagan belief, in a manner that was intended more to raise questions than to answer them definitively. How the questions were to be answered was being pointed at by the symbols on the cards themselves. For instance, The Pope and The Devil cards are very different from one another, yet the postures of the two are the same, and two people are seen below the main figure of each card. This would point to a connection of some sort because of the similarity of the situations depicted, but would not be readily noticed. The Pope with the two tonsured monks below him are similar to the Devil with the two chained individuals beneath him. Remember the Cathedral of Brandenburg, where a fox in priestly robes is preaching to a flock of geese? We have the same type of allusion here in the cards and it seems to point to the offices of the Pope and the Devil as being the same. We get more information about the early Tarot from a Latin manuscript written by a German monk named Johannes, in the year 1377. He describes the cards somewhat and it would seem that although the cards were evolved, they were not yet standardized. There were many more cards in the deck he speaks of, than in our modern Tarot deck. Johannes also seems to have noticed the possibility of using the cards for moral instruction. Whether he spread this idea to others, or if it was simply that others saw the possibility as well, is uncertain. What is certain is that the cards eventually became standardized and that standardization is centered on the idea of the four elements, or suits, and the various ways of combining them.

First Introduction of the Kabbala into the Tarot

The earliest Tarot deck still in existence is the Visconti-Sforza deck from about the mid-fifteenth century. In this deck, we can see that any evolution in the deck has now stopped, as the number of cards in the deck and the depictions in the cards then are the same as in modern-day packs. We can deduce from this that if there is a system underlying the Tarot, it was already in place at that time, because no major changes take place in their number or form afterwards. What does happen eventually is that a major change in the way the cards are interpreted takes place in the nineteenth century. This happens with the introduction of the Kabbala as a key to the symbolism in the cards. Court De Gebelin in the middle 1700s had mentioned this connection, but it was Eliphas Levi who made the firm link between the two systems. "In 1856 Eliphas Levi published *Le Dogme et Rituel de La Haute Magic*. Levi, whose real name was Alphonse Louis Constant, was the first writer to link the twenty-two Trump cards with the twenty-two letters of the Hebrew alphabet. He also linked the four suits in the card pack with the Tetragrammaton, the four Hebrew letters of Yod-He-Vau-He, usually translated as YHWH or JHVH (Yahweh or

Jehovah) and used as a substitute for the ineffable name of God." As we can see, this change in interpretation takes place roughly five hundred years after the first documentation of the cards. We have to ask ourselves then, if the creators of the cards originally intended this association, or was it later forced onto the cards by writers more comfortable with Judeo-Christian beliefs than the Pagan system of symbols the church first saw depicted in them. I say "forced," because the Kabbalistic symbols are often applied to different cards by different writers, so there is very little agreement as to how the Kabbala fits the Tarot's scheme.

If we look, at the classical cards, we find no hint as to any link with this Hebrew mystical system and yet the idea that they are tied together is a predominant belief among Tarot readers today and most likely a mistake. The sensibilities of the two systems are also in conflict, as Ronald O. Decker the art historian points out. "Another troubling mistake in popular occultism is the insistence that the Tarot, from Christian Italy, enshrines both Egyptian polytheism and Jewish monotheism. The theorists have never resolved the logical conflicts here. Jews in the Renaissance cannot have had much fondness for Christian or Egyptian symbols or for any 'graven images.' Most modern books on the Tarot uncritically assume that the Tarot's message is Kabbalistic. But even if Jewish Kabbalists had unaccountably embraced representational art, they would not likely have profaned their sacred wisdom by relegating it to playing cards...[8]" So why is this such a common theory today? The reasons I find are as follows: After Eliphas Levi wrote his book; there was an American Freemason named Albert Pike who appropriated large sections of Levi's works into his own book *Morals and Dogma*, which was intended for use by the Masonic Fraternity for instruction of its members. Pike's book was published in 1871 and this is some of what it said, "He who desires to attain to the understanding of the Grand Word and the possession of the Great Secret, ought carefully to

---

8 Clifton, Chas S. *Gnosis Magazine. Article: The Unexamined Tarot. Issue #18, page 44.*

read the Hermetic philosophers, and will undoubtedly attain initiation, as others have done; but he must take, for the key of their allegories, the single dogma of Hermes, contained in his table of Emerald, and follow, to class his acquisitions of knowledge and direct the operation, the order indicated in the Kabbalistic alphabet of the Tarot.[9]" This idea about the "Kabbalistic alphabet of the Tarot" then spread throughout the Masonic Fraternity. This organization then becomes the source for so many of the founders of the great many occult organizations that proliferated around, and during, the Victorian era.

In 1887, a very influential organization was born. This organization was called the Golden Dawn and three high-ranking Freemasons started it. It is this group that began a new revival of interest in things occult. From it sprang other groups and with them goes the idea that the Tarot is based on the Jewish

---

9 Pike, Albert. *Morals and Dogma of the Ancient and Accepted Scottish Rite of Freemasonry Prepared for the Supreme Council of the Thirty-third Degree, for the Southern Jurisdiction of the United States, and Published By Its Authority.* Charleston Southern Jurisdiction, 1919. P. 777.

Kabbala. This idea is now widespread in the occult community and can be traced back to one man, Eliphas Levi. Levi was a student and believer in the Kabbala and could therefore be said to see Kabbala everywhere, as Kabbalists are taught to do. It was on the slim coincidence that the Hebrew alphabet had twenty-two letters and the Tarot had the same number of cards in a portion of it that this association was made. I think this association was a real stretch. So, the situation today is such that the cards are being changed and redrawn to accommodate this foreign system. I believe this is causing us to lose the original meaning of the cards, and the heretical teaching hidden in its symbolism, through this later tampering.

In this book, I will avoid using modern decks, and use classical Tarot cards for our study. We will look at the symbols on the cards themselves and relate them strictly to the environment of their first appearance, fourteenth century Europe. This was the Europe, in which Paganism was in hiding and Christianity was the official state religion, that spawned the Tarot cards to hide a Pagan doctrine, almost in plain sight of the official state sponsored church.

The Need to Study the Tarot Cards in Light of its Origins

We will study the cards alone, without the addition of the system of the Kabbala, because it is based on premises that do not fit a Pagan faith. The Pagan and/or animistic faiths holds that all is divine, that the deities exist all around us as the forces of Nature.   This is in complete contradiction to the Kabbalistic system, that says we are in a fallen state and are totally separate from the divine. In fact, the Kabbalistic 'Tree of Life' illustrates how we are considered in that system, as so far removed from the Divine that the Godhead could not even directly create our world but instead manifested a series of intermediary states of being, known as 'sephira,' that would act as barriers to keep the Godhead free of our 'defiled' state of being, which is in the lowest 'sephira' Malkuth, at the very bottom of the 'tree.' Also, there six other levels above us that we could climb to come nearer to the deity, but we would still be held back from the ultimate knowledge of the "crown" by an abyss which keeps us in the lower parts of the tree of life.

What we will do instead is study the Tarot as it is. We will look for the patterns and symbols that are and have been in the cards since their origins and try to discern the 'hidden' Paganism that lies at its core. From this Pagan core, we will study our faith and see how the cards of the deck illustrate it.

The System of the Tarot

So, is there a system to the Tarot? If the Kabbala is not what the deck is based on, is there some other underlying system or pattern that we can detect? I believe that there is and that I have found it. Now, this search was not for things unknown. In other words, I was not searching for anything new, but instead, what I was looking for was a new way of combining things already known. This "combination of things" I believed was hidden in plain sight. If indeed the creators of the Tarot deck were smart enough to create the deck in the first place, then they must have been smart enough to place sufficient clues within the deck that someone using some deductive reasoning and common sense should be able to discover it.

I had some things going for me in this search. I had become interested in things hidden, or occult, at age fifteen; I am now fifty-eight. I am also an avid reader and have been reading this type of material constantly all these years. I was initiated into Freemasonry at the age of twenty-six; have achieved the thirty-second degree in the Scottish Rite and the seventh degree in the York Rite, as well as being initiated into the Shrine. So, I had been exposed to secret material that had a great deal of influence, in the past, on occult organizations and occult society in general. (See Appendix 3.)

I began to look for the pattern, in the cards, by accepting certain limitations to my search. First, I would not force anything onto the deck, which was not known at the time the deck came into existence. Second, I would accept the beliefs of the people, of that period, as valid and not try to rationalize them into something they were not. This would be the most difficult part of the process, as rationalization is something that human beings do almost subconsciously and I needed to guard against it. To prevent this from happening, I would have to historically validate all concepts and methods I related to the Tarot as having been known at the time of the deck's origin. I knew that the church did not condone the use of the cards and that it had very strong feelings about what the cards represented. Because of this, I looked to Pagan and heretical material existent at the time for more clues as to the cards' meanings.

The medieval belief was that everything was created from the four basic elements of fire, water, air, and earth. I could easily see these represented by the four suits in the Minor cards: staves, cups, swords, and coins. However, if it were true that "everything" was made up of these four elements, then, how were the "twenty-two" Trump cards derived from them?

The two, or is it three, arcanas?

Many different things had to come together in my mind, and over a decade devoted to this particular study, before that "aha" moment occurred and the secret spread started to reveal itself to me. It was Empedocles, around 450 B.C.E., that created this most enduring doctrine of "the four elements of earth, water, air and fire as the ultimate constituents of all things. To show how the different phenomena can be produced from these four, he gave the example of a painter who produces in two dimensions a varied world from the juxtaposition of a few colors.[10]" He taught that all material things were made up of these four elements, mingled in various proportions and influenced by two universal forces, "love" and "strife." These two "basic forces" were making their appearance in numerous places. They were appearing as "God and Goddess," as "attraction and repulsion," as "solve and coagula," "positive and negative," "properly and improperly placed," and so on, and on. It was becoming evident that the elements were being "acted" upon by these two forces and the forces may just have something to do with the "supposed" and "rumored" two Trump cards that were missing from the Tarot,

---

10 Wright, M. R. *Cosmology in Antiquity*. *Routledge, 1965. P.53.*

that make the twenty-four combinations possible with four elements, which I will explain more fully below.

The Tarot deck is normally described as being divided into two parts, the Major and Minor Arcana; the "Major Arcana" being the Trump cards and the "Minor Arcana" being the rest of the deck. This, however, does not seem to be the case in actual practice, such as is done when reading the cards. The Minor Arcana is usually divided into two parts as well, which are the pip and court cards, and each section of the deck is read, or interpreted, differently. The 22 major cards, the Trumps, are said to represent "divine" influences, the 16 court cards are interpreted as individual people and the 40 pip cards as mundane events or occurrences in the environment or situation around the person being read for. So we have three sets of numbers; 22, 16 and 40, that we should be able to derive from the number four which represents the number of elements. The three sections can also be attributed to the classical three worlds of upper, middle and lower realms, which are associated with the deities, humanity and the primal forces of the underworld, respectively. Adding these three numbers together is what gives us the total number of cards in any Tarot deck. So then, the question was how to derive the numbers.

There are legends in Freemasonry that the Masonic craft was brought to the West by a man named Peter Gower. Through my research, I had come to feel that Freemasonry was hiding, under the guise of Christianity and the Bible, a Pagan heart. Everything in Masonic ritual comes from biblical sources, but it was interesting to me that the selections of characters, even though they were from the bible, were either Pagan or Pagan-friendly and, if Pagan-friendly, had caused the god of the Old Testament to become annoyed with them for one reason or another. Masonic scholars have researched the name "Peter Gower" and have come up with the idea that it is an Anglicized version of the name Pythagoras. This is just the right trail to follow, because it is Pythagoras' system that is best known for studying the different permutations of the number four and had made the study of mathematics religious in nature and the basis for the Pythagorean religion. The tetractis, whose name means "four," is the most sacred symbol of the Pythagorean faith and looks like this:

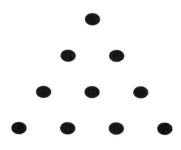

The Pythagorean Tetractis

"The importance of the Quaternary obtained by addition [that is to say $1 + 2 + 3 + 4$] is great in music because all the consonances are found in it. But it is not only for this reason that all Pythagoreans hold it in highest esteem: it is also because it seems to outline the entire nature of the universe. It is for this reason that the formula of their oath was: 'I swear by the one who has bestowed the Tetraktys to the coming generations, source of eternal nature, into our souls.'[11]" Some of the Pythagorean permutations of the number four are as follows:

$$1 \times 2 \times 3 \times 4 = 24$$
$$1 + 2 + 3 + 4 = 10$$
$$4 \times 10 = 40$$
$$4 \times 4 = 16$$

These calculations gave me the various sets of numbers that the three sections of the Tarot were comprised of. "The Pythagoreans introduced an important novelty in philosophy, the system of opposites. They compiled a table of what A. W. Benn called 'antithetical couples':

The Limited	And Unlimited
The One	And the Many
Rest	And Motion
Light	And Darkness
Good	And Evil

This notion of contrasts exerted a powerful influence in Greek thought. The Pythagoreans also launched the mystical notion that numbers and geometrical figures (mathematical forms)

---

11 *Guthrie, Kenneth S. The Pythagorean Sourcebook and Library. Phanes Press, Grand Rapids, Michigan, USA 1987. P. 317.*

are the immediate patterns from which all things are made. They held that the ultimate reality is a being that endures through all apparent changes. Being has seemingly dual existence in the form of unlimited space and numbers.[12]" Knowing this still did not give me any clue as to a pattern hidden within the deck, although it was this idea of "opposites" organized within "tables" that would eventually reveal the hidden side of the Tarot and the secret spread, for the entire system is based on it. It was a long and involved process that lead me to arriving at the pattern, so I will take each section in turn and explain how the pattern developed in each individual section. I will then combine the three sections and explain the entire pattern, and the relationships involved between the various cards.

---

12 Barnes, Harry Elmer. *An Intellectual and Cultural History of the Western World, Vol. One: From Earliest Times through the Middle Ages. Dover Publications, Inc., 1965. P.125.*

The Trump Cards

One day, I was reading a Masonic encyclopedia and I saw an illustration of the four cardinal virtues. The virtues had representing them four images of young women and the names of the virtues were underneath them. As I looked at these, it occurred to me that the illustrations seemed almost like Tarot cards. Then I realized that, except for a slight variation in word usage, these virtues were the same virtues illustrated in the cards. This in itself was not a great revelation, since other authors had also noticed that the four cardinal virtues were depicted in the Tarot. It was this simple observation, however, that lead me into a train of thought that would reveal the Tarot's hidden structure.

The virtues in the Masonic book were named: Fortitude, Temperance, Justice and Prudence. Of course, the meanings of the words were the same as the four words describing the virtues in the Tarot deck and the interchange of words would be a natural occurrence, especially if someone were translating the words from another language, as was done with the cards. So then the four cardinal virtues or, as they have been referred to as well, Pagan Virtues, were as follows: Fortitude was Strength in the Tarot deck, Justice was the same, Temperance the same, and Prudence was called Judgment.

So, the four Pagan virtues were illustrated in the Tarot deck. Having previously looked at the permutations of the number four, regarding the deck, I wondered if there were other significant groupings of four in the Trump cards and, lo and behold, there were! As I laid out all the Trump cards of the Tarot out in front of me, I noticed next that there were four planetary or celestial cards. Now some of the cards would not be seen as planets today, however, at the time of the first appearance of the Tarot in Europe, they were.

The World card was the planet earth, this was obvious enough, the sun was considered one of the planets back then, as was the moon, but what about the Star card? That's when Freemasonry gave me some more clues as to where to look. In Freemasonry, one of the most important symbols is what is known as the "Blazing Star." Reading more Masonic literature I found that a "blazing star" is called "blazing" because the star passes through the rays of the sun. The morning and evening star does exactly this as the two stars are really just one and it is the planet Venus. I will explain more about the association of the Star card to Venus later. So, we have four planets in the deck as follows: "The World" was earth, Sun and Moon, plus "The Star" was the planet Venus or the "morning and evening star." I now had two sets of four, the virtues and the planets, which defined four of the "celestial spheres." I next looked for other "sets of four" in the trump cards.

The next set of four I noticed, I called the "authorities." The original reason I noticed them is that, of all the actual people depicted in the Trump cards, only four were sitting on thrones perched on daises. It was this clue that leads me to find this set. Sitting on thrones were "The Emperor," "The Empress," "The Hierophant" and "The High Priestess." In all decks the names of the "Emperor" and "Empress" remain the same, however, the names of the two other cards change from one deck to another. The meanings, though, in all decks remain essentially the same. The "Hierophant" can be called "the Pope" or "the High Priest" as well, which matched up with his "mate" the "High Priestess" which has also been called "the Popess" or in French "la Papesse." So this set of four represented the ruling class, or authorities, in the culture of the middle ages, although it added a common legend of the era, that of a female pope, to make the four symmetrical, male to female, and bringing the number to four.

The next set of four I called the "uncontrollable forces." I was looking at the "lightning struck tower" card and noticed a similarity between it and the "lovers" card. In each card, something above was "striking" or about to strike something below. In the case of the "tower" card, a bolt of lightning was striking a building, and in the case of the "lovers" card, Cupid was about to shoot an arrow at the male figure in the card. I looked for other cards that depicted an influence from above toward something, or someone below, but found none.

The deck I was using was the Visconti-Sforza, which, if you remember, is the oldest deck known to still exist. In reading about it, I found that the original Tower card had been lost and the modern publisher had drawn a new card to replace it. This replacement depiction of the Tower card was not therefore untainted by modern innovation and would not have the subtle symbolism used in the original cards. So, looking closer at the Lovers card I noticed a blindfold on the cupid figure above. I looked for other cards with blindfolds on them and came up with the Wheel of Fortune and Death cards. This is when I noticed that in all three of these cards the subject was a force said to be beyond the control of any particular individual. This was very definitely about something "uncontrollable."

Just think about a roulette wheel and how often gamblers would like to be able to control the outcome of just such a wheel. Well, here it was, depicted for us in the cards. This time, however, there were positioned around the wheel different classes of people, such as rich, poor, old and young. Think about your fate; how in control is anyone really concerning their fate? Even the station in life into which you were born is part of a person's fate. How in control are we as to who our parents are or whether or not we will be born rich or poor, to intelligent parents or to a couple of unintelligent morons, so to speak. No control whatsoever! That is what the "wheel" card represents. It is the "luck of the draw" and the cards we are dealt by simply being born into this life, and it is totally out of our control what those cards will be. We must simply "play" the hand dealt to us and make the best of it. I remembered another name the card had been called, and that was the "Wheel of Fate," and right in the middle of the wheel, at the hub, was a figure blindfolded. The blindfold was evidently symbolic for the inability to see, or foresee, the future result of the force at work in the card.

What about the Death card? When death will come to any individual is anyone's guess. Death is the great uncontrollable force for all of us. Some may try and take control from death by trying to commit suicide, but even then, there is no guarantee; suicides are often prevented by unforeseen circumstances. The very curious thing about the image on the Death card was the position of the blindfold. The Wheel and Lovers cards had blindfolds directly over the eyes of the figure representing the "force" of the card, but not so with the Death card. The skeletal figure very definitely had a blindfold on, but it was raised up above its eye sockets. Why was this? Did it mean that "death" itself could see when it performed its deadly task, or was it that it alone of the three figures had no eyes, and so, required no blindfold except for its symbolic value which linked it with the other cards in this group?

The Lovers, the Wheel of Fortune and the Death cards, made three of the four "uncontrollable force" cards; so what was the last one? Was it the first card that I had looked at, the Lightning Struck Tower? The original card was lost, so it was unknown as to whether or not a blindfolded figure had been depicted on it, but the force in the card was unmistakable. The card had also been called "the House of

God," and God was definitely at work in the card with what insurance companies today call an "act of God." The card represents that which surrounds us at all times, the forces of Nature and the "acts of God" as being destructive.

Now, there were six Trump cards left on the table in front of me. Two of the six were the Magician and Fool cards, and four others, which were "the hermit," "the chariot," "the hanged man" and "the devil" cards. I found these six cards presented quite a puzzle for me. The Magician and Fool seemed to be opposites to one another, as the Magician, also known as the Juggler or in French "le Bateleur" was skilled, smart, wise and so on, and this was the exact opposite of the "fool." These cards were the alpha and omega, if you will, of a person's life into which we are born, as a "babe in the woods," ignorant of life's ways and we go out at the end of that life, more skilled, knowledgeable, and hopefully, wiser than we came into it. So, if I took the Fool and Magician cards out of the mix, because I was seeing them as the beginning and end of a journey, then it left four cards. How were these last four to be classed?

I am sometimes amazed at how the brain works and makes these leaps of logic, or maybe association, as it did in this case. I was looking at the Hanged Man card when I remembered an occurrence in my life from fifth grade. I was taking a test, and evidently I had not studied at all, because I was sitting at my desk and nothing was coming. Every time I read a question I just sat there, probably with a very confused look on my face, and waited, hoping for some kind of answer to the question to magically appear, but it did not. The teacher said something to me in French and I looked up at her even more confused, because I didn't speak French. She then told me that when she was a little girl in France, if you didn't know the answer to a question and just waited, like I was doing, for something to come to mind then it was said, "You are hanging out to dry." Well there I was, "hanging out to dry," waiting, doing nothing, just waiting; the Hanged Man was doing nothing just waiting there on the card. Then the word popped into my head "phlegmatically!" The Hanged Man was the picture of the humor "phlegm." I looked at the other three cards and they clicked into place; they were the four humors. Choleric is fiery, mean and quick to anger, the Devil card; melancholy is withdrawn and pensive, the Hermit card; sanguine is triumphant and joyful, such as a hero in a triumphal chariot during the Roman era, the Chariot card; and then of course, the first humor that hit me, phlegm is lazy and doing nothing, hanging out to dry, the Hanged Man. This set, of four cards, represented the four humors. The Trump cards had divided very nicely into five sets of four, with two cards left over. However, the question remained, "Why not six sets of four?"

The Elements

Reading about the Tarot, I came across a reference to the "Docters Van Leeuwen Porcelain Tarot" in the "Encyclopedia of the Tarot" by Stuart Kaplan. This Tarot deck had something, which no other deck had, and that was all the possible combinations of four different letters.

The letters were the ones that spell Tarot without the last "t." So some of the combinations were "TARO, ROTA, TORA and so on. There were twenty-four combinations representing twenty-four trump cards, not the twenty-two we have in the Tarot today. Docters Van Leeuwen's theory was that the church tried to ban the Tarot in 300 c.e. and only succeeded in eliminating two cards, those that represented the ultimate male and female principles and also that the different permutations of the letters in the word "taro" created words which gave meaning to the cards themselves. Not all of this made sense to me. Why would the church have succeeded in eliminating only two cards and still leave the major portion of the deck with no mention ever, by anyone, of the two cards, and no attempt ever to re-instate them? In addition, the words created by the permutations were a bit of a stretch in some cases and then had to be in a wide variety of languages to make any sense. I felt that a small group of letters in any random combination would make a word in some language somewhere, if spelled phonetically.

Therefore, I did not buy the whole theory, but it did give me an idea.

What if, instead of the letters of the word "taro," we used the suits themselves representing the four elements? Doing this, we arrive at the same twenty-four possible combinations. This would fit nicely with the Pythagorean equation $1 \times 2 \times 3 \times 4 = 24$. However, as I said, there are only twenty-two Trump cards. I later found out that the two blank cards "traditionally" left in a deck of Tarot cards had more to do with the printing process than someone intentionally making them blank to hide something. These two cards simply rounded off the number of cards from seventy-eight to eighty, which is easier to print. I did not want to add any cards to the current deck, as Docters Van Leeuwen had done, but instead wanted to find the reason for the cards' number and structure as they are. So, the next question was which two combinations of elements would logically be left unassigned to any card, and then, why? I thought of the Pagan deities and the fact that these Gods and Goddesses were not infallible. They were not absolutely good or bad, but had all the very human foibles we all have. They had very distinctive personalities. There was the clue, personalities! Personalities were thought to be a function of the elements as they responded to the dictates of the body. "The body, says Hippocrates, is compounded of blood, phlegm, yellow bile, and black bile; that man enjoys the most perfect health in whom these elements are duly proportioned and mingled; pain is the defect or excess of one 'humor,' or its isolation from the rest." So, if a Tarot trump card was representing an individual or deity, then it would also have a personality composed of the four elements and there would be twenty-four personalities in the deck derived from all the possible combinations of these four elements. Now, how to classify elements in any particular combination as having a defect or being in excess?

"Aristotle conceived of the universe as having the earth--a stationary sphere--at its center. Around it, revolve some fifty-five concentric and transparent spheres, on which the moon, sun, planets, and moving stars are placed. All is surrounded by the great sphere or primum mobile, beyond which God dwells among the fixed stars. God, as prime mover, set the whole in motion, and all heavenly motion is circular and eternal.

Aristotle's physical theories were based upon the doctrine adopted from Empedocles that all earthly objects are composed of the four fundamental elements--earth, air, fire, and water. The heavenly bodies are made of the mysterious fifth element, ether.[13]" Aristotle had also said that the elements could be "properly placed." If this was true then it could also be said that elements can be "improperly" placed. This gave me the idea of a "positive" and "negative" influence on any one particular element. This also coincided with Empedocles' teaching of "two great antagonistic forces." "The elements then were to be understood to be subject to the opposed forces of Love and Strife working on

---

13 Barnes, Harry Elmer. *An Intellectual and Cultural History of the Western World, Vol. One: From Earliest Times through the Middle Ages. Dover Publications, Inc., 1965. P.144.*

them with expanding and contracting areas of application as they were brought together or held further apart. In Empedocles' theory the tensions of such attraction and repulsion resulted in the repeated patterns of movements and arrangements of the elements within the cosmos, in the genesis and destruction of successive generations of mortal life and, for individuals, in friendships and enmities.[14]"

The elements are assigned, in a variety of traditions, to different directional quadrants so that fire might be assigned to the south, water to the north, and so on. Because of this, you could assign the elements to a particular direction and consider them "properly" placed, or you could mixed them up and some would be properly placed and others not. I needed to decide which compass directions would best suit each element, so that I could call this position "proper." In addition, I needed to make a decision about the relationship of the elements to the cardinal directions on the compass. I

---

14 Wright, M. R. *Cosmology in Antiquity. Routledge, 1965. P.99.*

decided that alchemy had the best way of relating the elements to each other, because it did so according to the physical qualities each possessed. Fire had the qualities "hot and dry," water; "cold and moist," air; "moist and hot," and earth; "dry and cold." Now "dry" could be considered the opposite of "moist" and "hot" the opposite of "cold." This coincided with the qualities Aristotle had assigned to them. So, I placed them on a circle, representing a compass, with a relationship to one another like this:

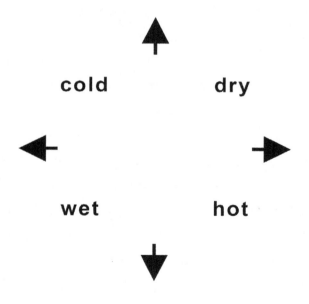

Once this was done, it was easy enough to place two of the elements into their proper quadrants on the compass, keeping in mind that the south was the place of greatest heat due to the sun's maximum strength being there, and north was the direction that produce cold and wet in the form of snow, hail, sleet, etc. Therefore, I placed the element of fire in the south and the element of water in the north. This left two other elements to place correctly; earth and air. Which belonged in the east and which the west? The east is the direction of the "birth" of the sun and moon. The west is the direction of their "death." Looking for some way to assign these elements to the appropriate direction led me to thinking about the seasons of the year for some kind of clue. Summer was the hottest season and so could be related to fire. Winter was the coldest and wettest season and would relate to water nicely. So, what happens in the spring and fall? Well, in the spring the earth comes back to life with new foliage and new buds are springing forth everywhere. This is also the time most animals have their young.

The fall, on the other hand, has to do with death. The leaves on the tree wither and die, many trees becoming as skeletons with no leaves on them at all. So the question came down to 'what was life and death to people of the fourteenth century? How were these symbolized and how could this relate to a compass direction?

It was fairly obvious that spring was the season associated with birth and fall with death. East was the place of birth, because of where the sun and moon come into our field of awareness and west was the place of death because that is where they leave and go in to the underworld; the land of the dead. The biggest clue I had about relating an element to these directions was that life was considered present if the person or animal was breathing and considered dead if they were not. Even the word "spirit" comes from the Latin 'espiritus' which means "breath." From ancient times, birds had been considered messengers from that other world and was even reflected in that old saying, "a little bird told me" and many omens were brought by different kinds of birds. Birds, of course, are creatures of the air. When a person dies, their spirit leaves them, they no longer breathe, and that spirit goes to the place of death; the land of spirits. The place of death is the west; this had to be where spirits went. This is even reflected in the "Necropolis" of ancient Egypt being on the western side of the Nile.

Therefore, going on these assumptions I placed the elements as follows: fire in the south, water in the north, earth in the east and air in the west. This arrangement of elements produced this:

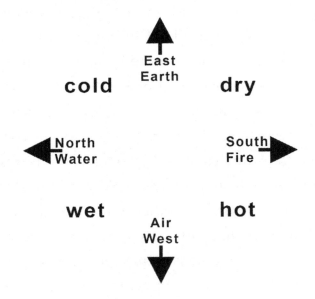

This seemed to be a nice arrangement. None of the qualities that were considered antagonistic were next to each other, they were on opposite sides of the circle, and it related to the seasons well. Then, just out of curiosity, I decided to look at the zodiacal signs associated with each of the seasons. I knew that Claudius Ptolemy was the person that decided to 'regularize the distribution' of elements to the signs, but this distribution had always seemed arbitrary to me. For example: "the water bearer" Aquarius is assigned the element of air, Aries, the ram is assigned to fire (what does a ram have to do with fire?) and Scorpio (which is represented by three animals; the scorpion, eagle and serpent) was assigned to water. If you look closely, you will see that Ptolemy simply went around the circle of the signs assigning elements to them by alternating fire, earth, air, water, fire, earth, air, water, fire, earth, air, water, all the way around the circle, without considering either the image of the sign, or the season the sign was in. As Rupert Gleadow writes about the sign Virgo after Ptolemy's reassignment, "it is far indeed from the pretty maid of fifteen who was the original symbol. The pretty maid was an angel -- she had wings. She represented Astraea, the goddess or heavenly power of Justice, who dwelt on earth in the Golden Age. No wonder that her natives were described as the most helpful and charming in the zodiac! But Ptolemy, when he made Virgo a sign of Earth, could not help but cut off her wings; so now we are presented with this cold, selfish, viperish old maid![15]" However, if you look at the signs of any particular season, using common sense and not ignoring the actual images associated with them, you will find something entirely different from what Ptolemy told us was there.

The signs of winter are Capricorn, Aquarius and Pisces. Look at their pictures! Capricorn, a fishtailed creature; Aquarius, the water bearer and Pisces, two fish! What can be more apparent than this? Fish tail, water, and two fish. It was obvious that the season of winter should be associated with the element water by looking at

---

15 Gleadow, Rupert. *The Origin of the Zodiac. Atheneum, NY, 1969. P.42.*

the signs of the season. Winter is the season, to put it quite simply, when 'cold and wet' happens in the form of rain, snow, sleet, and hail.

The signs of fall are Libra, Scorpio and Sagittarius. These took a bit more study, as did some of the other signs in other seasons, to crack the elemental code of the zodiac. Libra is the weighing 'scales,' and it is the sun sign right after the Autumnal Equinox, which is when the days become shorter than the nights, and so, the God is said to have died. Looking back at the origins of the zodiac, I find Osiris dies and goes into the underworld to be the judge of the dead. He has before him the scales which he will use to pass judgment. The land of the dead is in the west; associated with the fall season. The first sign of this season is Libra the scales, and Osiris' heart, that is the heart of the dead person, who is now called Osiris, is weighed against the weight of a feather on these same scales. Notice, Libra has to do with the weight of a feather, that is 'light as air.' The dead must have less guilt in their heart than the weight of a feather for them to be judged worthy and not be thrown to the hippopotamus to be devoured. Scorpio has three animals that are associated with it, an eagle (a creature of the air) and two poisonous animals, the scorpion and snake, which remove the spirit, or breath, from a person with their sting and bite. Then finally, Sagittarius the archer shooting an arrow, with its feathered flocking, into the air. Three signs and all their pictures related to the element air. This was fitting nicely with my assignment of elements to cardinal points of the compass.

Now, to move on the signs of spring, which are Aries, Taurus and Gemini. I was trying to stay consistent and simply look at the images of the signs and use common sense, but here, I was a bit perplexed. It was not until I started to recall the actual living creatures associated with the signs that something clicked. Aries was a ram, an animal that is distinctive because when it is about to charge, to "ram" something with its horns, it bows its head to the earth and scrapes the ground, kicking back dust and dirt, before it does so. Taurus the bull does exactly the same thing right before it charges. Two animals, both bow their heads to the ground, scrape it and kick up dirt behind them right before charging. I could see how primitive association could relate these two animals with the earth. However, what about Gemini? How did Gemini relate to the element earth? This was the third sign of the spring season and I could not see any apparent connections between twins and the earth.

Doing some more research on ancient deities, I found that "twin deities" are prominent in a great many cultures. The interesting thing about these "twin gods" is that they are, in almost all cases, opposites of one another in some important way. For example: Castor and Pollux are opposite to one another because one is mortal and the other immortal. Even though opposite to each other in some way, there is one detail about twins that cannot escape being noticed, the fact that they look the same. It is almost as if they were one person in two bodies. When twins are seen separately, a person may not even be aware which of the pair is in front of them. In the case of Castor and Pollux, Castor dies, but is loved so much by Pollux that Pollux makes a deal with Zeus. Pollux wishes to share his immortality with his brother and a deal is struck to enable each to live sequentially with the other. The two brothers are never seen together again; when Castor is living, Pollux is dead and visa versa, and so they move back and forth from living on earth to being dead in Hades. What these twins seem to be alluding to is an individual human being, that contains within him or herself two beings, one mortal and the other not. These two beings would represent the body and soul of the individual. In her book *Mythology*, Edith Hamilton places these twins gods in the group she calls "gods of the earth." The Greek gods were classified according to their residence or location. They either belonged in Olympus, which was heaven, in the oceans, seas and rivers, in the underworld or on the earth. The twins were of those deities of earth and this sign, therefore, related to earth because of who these gods were. Therefore, Aries, Taurus and Gemini lined up well with the element of earth.

The signs of summer are Cancer, Leo and Virgo. Looking at these three signs, I could see immediately how Leo the lion could be associated with fire. The very look of a male lion, with its fiery orange color and mane emanating from its head like the rays of light from the sun; the image fit. Cancer, though, took a little more searching. I found that the sign was called "the crab" through an error that had been perpetuated down through the ages. Cancer had originally been "the scarab" when the zodiac was first created; through drawing and re-drawing the scarab, it had mutated into a crab. The scarab was the beetle that, in ancient Egypt, was said to push the sun across the sky each day. Therefore, it was readily apparent that as a scarab, it related to the element of fire easily because it pushed the sun. However, even if the sign were to simply remain a crab, it should still be associated to the sun and fire. This is because the crab sign is said to be in the place it is in the zodiac because, at this time of year, right at the summer Solstice, the sun is said to 'walk backward' like a crab; we're still talking about the sun here and fire again. Virgo was much more difficult to deal with. What does a virgin have to do with fire? However, things were not as simple as all that. She is not just a virgin; she is the virgin of the cornfields. Now if you have ever lived near cornfields, you know that at the time of year when the sun is in Virgo, it is time to harvest the corn. Just like leaves that turn red in the fall, corn when ready to harvest is the same color as the lion; fiery orange to red and when the corn moves in the wind it looks like fire is moving across the fields. I have lived near just such cornfields and it is a beautiful sight. This was the only association I could come up with for Virgo. Did ancient man come up with the same association? I'm not sure. I do know that ancient man's associations had less to do with what they read in a book and more to do with what they saw in the world around them, and cornfields do have this fiery look to them at this time of year. Therefore, I related these three signs all to fire.

The signs were lining up, in the main, with the elements as I had placed them on the wheel of the year and the points of the compass. The actual pictures of the zodiac corroborated the placement of the elements in the alchemical fashion of opposite qualities being placed across the circle and everything appeared to fit a "proper placement" like this:

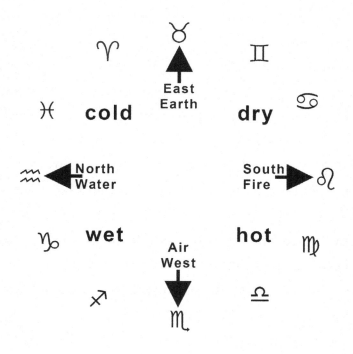

The seasons of the year would then be placed, with their signs, as follows: spring in the east, summer in the south, fall in the west and winter in the north. This placement was verified by another source, a book on star-gazing, that pointed out the fact that the handle of the 'Big Dipper,' if looked at in the early evening, points east during the spring, south during the summer, west during the fall and north during the winter. This would seem to be the best placement for the elements on the compass points. (See Appendix 1, for a comparison between this 'common sense' pictorial approach to assigning elements to zodiacal signs and the arbitrary assignment of Claudius Ptolemy.)

I now had in place a way to consider a particular direction as the "proper placement" for any particular element. A suit representing fire placed in the south would be strengthened, because "hot and dry" is added to "hot and dry," so the qualities already present in the suit are increased. On the other hand, a suit representing water, which is "cold and wet," placed in the same quadrant would be diminished as "hot" lessens "cold" and "dry" lessens "wet" and would be considered "improperly placed." This method of placement also allowed for elements to be neutrally placed, such as air which is "hot and wet" being placed in the water quadrant which has the qualities of "cold and wet," thereby strengthening one quality while weakening the other, and so, having a total null effect on the element.

The question remained though, had two cards been removed from the deck, as Docters Van Leeuwen had suggested when he created his deck with twenty-four Trump cards? Was there another reason for two combinations of four elements not to be represented by the cards? In order to try and answer these questions, I used the four Ace cards of each suit to represent each element. I made every combination of Aristotle's "proper placement" of elements. There are twenty-four possible combinations of four elements as we saw above: $1 \times 2 \times 3 \times 4 = 24$. I associated elements with the four cardinal directions, and by changing the elements in these directions, each individual element can be classified as "properly placed" or not. In making all the combinations of four elements, I realized that one combination was "perfect" in that every element was exactly in its best possible position. At the same time, there was another combination that was its exact opposite in that every element was in exactly its worst possible position. These two combinations were the extremes in terms of polarity. They were the antagonistic forces of Empedocles, perfect in their extremes and not represented by any card.

Pagan deities have personalities along with the strengths and weaknesses inherent with having those personalities. Just like people, none of the Pagan deities are perfect, neither perfectly right nor perfectly wrong. Perfect good and perfect evil were concepts applied by Christians to their God and their devil, they were not concepts related to any Pagan deity. Pagan deities had "personalities." They had relationships with one another, strengths and weaknesses in their makeup. None of them would have been called "perfect" good or bad and these two combinations of cards in which the elements were perfectly placed as "good" and "bad" were not represented by a card or a deity. Removing these two combinations left the twenty-two combinations that would relate to the Trump cards we are familiar with in the Tarot. These twenty-two cards represented a continuum, by degree, between the two extremes not in the cards, of totally "perfect placement" and totally "imperfect placement."

Combination of Elements Describe a Personality

So then, we now have the quadrants associated with individual elements and we have the elements themselves relating to one another as follows:

- Fire traits are strengthened in the fire quadrant, diminished in the water, and unaltered in the earth or air quadrant.

- Water traits are strengthened in the water quadrant, diminished in the fire, and unaltered in the earth or air quadrant.

- Air traits are strengthened in the air quadrant, diminished in the earth, and unaltered in the fire or water quadrant.

• Earth traits are strengthened in the earth quadrant, diminished in the air, and unaltered in the fire or water quadrant.

Creating a table, with the first four columns representing the compass directions, with all possible placements of the four elements in each column, I was easily able to see whether or not an element was strengthened, diminished or left unaltered by its placement. I made a fifth column in the table, in which I used a plus sign to show 'strengthened,' a negative to show 'diminished' and a zero to show no effect. This is what the table looks like:

South	North	West	East	Effect
fire	water	air	earth	+ + + +
fire	water	earth	air	+ + - -
fire	air	earth	water	+ 0 - 0
fire	air	water	earth	+ 0 0 +
fire	earth	water	air	+ 0 0 -
fire	earth	air	water	+ 0 + 0
water	air	earth	fire	- 0 - 0
water	air	fire	earth	- 0 0 +
water	earth	fire	air	- 0 0 -
water	earth	air	fire	- 0 + 0
water	fire	air	earth	- - + +
water	fire	earth	air	- - - -

South	North	West	East	Effect
air	earth	fire	water	0 0 0 0
air	earth	water	fire	0 0 0 0
air	fire	water	earth	0 - 0 +
air	fire	earth	water	0 - - 0
air	water	earth	fire	0 + - 0
air	water	fire	earth	0 + 0 +
earth	fire	water	air	0 - 0 -
earth	fire	air	water	0 - + 0
earth	water	air	fire	0 + + 0
earth	water	fire	air	0 + 0 -
earth	air	fire	water	0 0 0 0
earth	air	water	fire	0 0 0 0

My next question was how to assign a particular combination of elements to one particular card. I started with twenty-four combinations, removed the two that were "perfectly right" and "perfectly wrong" by taking out the two combinations with four plus and four minus signs. These two combinations could be considered the pair of opposites that Empedocles called "love" and "strife." This left me with twenty-two combinations; twenty of these relating to humors, planets, authorities, virtues and fates, leaving the two last cards, which were "the Fool" and "the Magician."

Leaving these two out of consideration for the moment, the other twenty Trump cards needed to be grouped into their associated elements.

The Humors

The humors were easy enough. Much had been written about which elements they were linked with, so I simply used that in the following manner:

Fire/South	Water/North	Air/West	Earth/East
Choleric	Phlegm	Sanguine	Melancholy
The Devil	The Hanged Man	The Chariot	The Hermit

The Devil card, representing the humor choleric, is easily recognized as having a fiery temper and being quick to anger. In addition, in traditional literature the devil is said to reside in a region of fire. So, The Devil card representing the humor choleric is assigned to the element fire.

The Hanged Man card, representing the humor phlegm, is waiting, doing nothing. What is he waiting for? Well, in his posture of hanging, he is waiting for death. He is being subjected to a method of execution, which is both time-consuming and painful. Hanging upside down, the blood eventually pools in the head and swells the brain until death occurs. All that is left for him to do is, wait. Strangely, the Hanged Man is often represented as being near water, or hanging over a pool of water. This may have to do with the method of execution. Eventually the blood, having pooled in the head to such an extent that it kills the person, will begin to bleed out of the ears, eyes and mouth, thus creates a pool of blood beneath the person. This blood can be viewed as the water of the body and, therefore, a pool of water near the Hanged Man. I did surmise, later, that the body of water could be considered a "reflecting pool," and the reflection of the Hanged Man in the pool was part of the clues to the "secret pattern" of the Tarot, which I will explain more fully in the final chapter of this book. Therefore, we assign the Hanged Man and phlegm to the element water.

The Chariot card, representing the humor sanguine, is the triumphal chariot of the conquering hero being welcomed back after his excursions. It is not the "war chariot" but instead the "parading chariot" in which the hero rides joyously down the street to the cheers of the crowd. The sun as the chariot in a journey across the sky is representative of a human life with all its travails. At the end of that journey is celebration and joy. As the sun sets in the west, the place of death and air, it has come to the end of the road and now all there is left to do is be happy about the end of struggle and hardship; to celebrate a life well lived. The Chariot card is not about the journey, or the battle, but their end and the west, which is associated with the element air.

The Hermit card, representing the humor melancholy, is the old man looking back on his life seeking to understand the meaning of it all. He withdraws and goes inward into his own thoughts, becoming more spiritual and pensive. He is the Hermit who goes to live in a cave and be alone. The cave, the heaviness of depression and melancholy are like the heaviness of the earth and so assigned to that element; earth.

The Celestial Spheres

Fire/South	Water/North	Air/West	Earth/East
The Sun	The Moon	The Star	The World

Assigning the planets to the different elements was fairly straightforward. The sun is easily associated with fire. The moon and its relationship with the tides was put into the group associated with water. The world, which is even called "earth," has to do with the physical plane and the element earth. These three being so easily assigned to their respective elements left the Star card, which had to be related to air, but how?

What were the "ancients" thinking about the Star and the remaining element air? This is where I began to wonder exactly which "star" was being referenced in the card. Modern "Star" cards have taken to placing seven smaller stars around the one main star and this would make the star refer to the North Star or Pole Star, because of the seven stars in the Big Dipper that circle it. However, if we look at the earlier "Star" cards we find that there was only one star depicted on them. This star was being associated with a beautiful young woman, also depicted in the card. Once we eliminate the Pole star as a possibility, we have two other mythologically important stars to choose from. Important because of their brightness and because of ancient man having to rely only on his ability to see the stars with his eyes, having nothing like a telescope at the time, and so, these two stars stood out from the rest. One of these is Sirius and the other would be the planet Venus. Sirius is known as the "Dog Star" and this does not seem to relate at all to the beautiful young lady; however, Venus does. Venus, although technically a planet, fits the criteria of star because the word "planet" means "wandering star." These "wandering stars" were, in the world of the Tarot's origin, considered "stars," and this star related well to the image of a "beautiful young woman." Also, this planet was known by another name, "Lucifer," who was called "prince of air" by John Milton in "Paradise Lost." Even though Milton was born roughly three hundred years after the origin of the Tarot, he was making a reference to the passage in Ephesians 2:2 where it says, "Wherein in time past ye walked according to the course of this world, according the prince of the power of the air, the spirit that now worketh in the children of disobedience." This would pin down the card to the element air and the planet Venus as "Morning and Evening Star" quite well. However, as I looked at the card, I noticed that the woman in the picture was pouring water from two pitchers into a river or lake. I did a search for references to any image of pouring water, a river, and a goddess. What I found was "the Styx Oath." "Any Immortal who pours the waters of Styx, and swears an oath, is solemnly bound to tell only the truth. The punishment for breaking such an oath is one year without ambrosia, nectar or AIR![16]" The image was a reference to the river that separated the world of

---

16 http://mythagora.com/bios/styx.html

the living from the underworld, or land of the dead. Again, this related the card to the west and air. So, the four planets depicted in the Tarot's Trump Cards are: Sun, Moon, Venus and Earth. The very same planets that Alexander, in his *Commentary on Aristotle's Metaphysics*, equates with the first three proportions to produce the "music of the spheres." The distances he suggests are based on that of the moon from the earth, with the sun twice that far, Venus three times, Mercury four times and the others in similar arithmetic proportion.[17] Therefore, the four planets of the Tarot define the three celestial spheres closest to our world.

The Authorities

Fire/South	Water/North	Air/West	Earth/East
The Emperor	The Empress	High Priestess	High Priest

The Emperor card is the embodiment of the conquering warrior. As emperor, he rules over

---

17 Wright, M. R. *Cosmology in Antiquity.* Routledge, 1965. P.136.

an empire that is, by definition, an extensive territory or a number of territories or nations that is ruled by a single supreme authority. The emperor would be that single supreme authority. How did he become an emperor? By means of war, in which one territory after another is consumed by its fire. In fact, once humanity mastered fire it became one of the chief weapons of war and has been used since antiquity for the purpose. Just like a fire, the Emperor wages war, consumes and destroys land, and property, as his dominion spreads. The Emperor is therefore assigned to the element fire.

The Empress in the Tarot is usually depicted as pregnant, although in some decks there may be some debate about this. She is the picture of womanhood and represents the female gender in its archetypal role. The woman is associated with water and moisture, because of the way the female body functions. The woman bleeds monthly once she has reached maturity, moisture is present when a woman becomes sexually aroused, "water breaks" when she is about to give birth and she lactates after the child is born. The female body would seem to produce liquid of one sort or another a large part of the time. We therefore assign the Empress as the epitome of femininity to the element water.

The High Priestess is normally represented sitting in front of two pillars. These two pillars are the pillars on a porch of an ancient temple. She may hold a book or scroll in her lap and she is usually veiled. What she is symbolizing is the mysteries of death, for she guards the gate between the world of the living and the world of the dead. The book she holds is "knowledge" in a general way, but also knowledge specifically of that which all people have always wondered about; what happens once we pass through that gate into the other world of the dead? The Priestess holds that secret. To look upon her face is to know her and her mystery. The veil also recalls the veil of the old wedding ceremony that is not lifted until the marriage is officially declared, and then the kiss and the ceremony is at its end. She is the guardian by which the spirit will pass after the body no longer breathes.

She is in the west and is assigned to the element air.

The Pope or High Priest is then assigned to the element earth. He oversees the rituals and expounds on "the laws" of God. What do the laws pertain to? They are about the living of one's life. What is "right" and what is "wrong" in the eyes of God; he tells people this. He is all about our actions in this material world. He tells us what rituals must be performed, how they should be performed, what our duties are, not only to God, but also, to our society, and our families. The High Priest's focus is all on the physical world and our life here as a preparation for the afterlife. His domain is the element of earth.

The Virtues

Fire/South	Water/North	Air/West	Earth/East
Strength	Temperance	Justice	Judgement

Assigning elements to the virtues began with the card "Temperance," which was fairly straightforward. In the Temperance card, we see a woman pouring a liquid from one pitcher into another. In my readings, I had come across the idea of tempering wine. In ancient times, wine was not drunk the way we do today. Wine drunk "untempered" was considered barbaric, and therefore was "tempered" before drinking by mixing some water into it. Of course, the ability to temper wine properly was considered a skill of refinement and proper etiquette, since mixing too much water into the wine could have been construed as miserly, and mixing in too little as uncouth. The virtue of temperance is knowing the difference between too little and too much. Being temperate is doing, for any particular situation, what is "appropriate," and so, "just right." The Temperance card's image, having to do with the mixing of liquids, I assigned to the element water.

The Strength card was also easily assigned. The lion in the card associated the card with the zodiacal sign "Leo" and the hot summer months when it is in its ascendancy. The lion is also associated with the sun, as I have already mentioned, because of its fiery color and mane.

Therefore, I assigned the Strength card as the virtue of fire.

The Judgment card shows what appears to be the "Last Judgment." People's bodies are being resurrected from their graves to the trumpet call of the angel Gabriel. God's "wrath is come, and the time of the dead, that they should be judged, and that thou shouldest give reward unto thy servants the prophets, and to the saints, and them that fear thy name, small and great; and shouldest destroy them which destroy the earth."

It is important to remember, it is during the time of the first Tarot decks that Pagan and Christian beliefs are being blended and mixed together, to give voice to the ancient Pagan teachings through the medium of the relatively new Christian religion. In the Judgment card, we have an excellent example of this syncretic process. Bodies, that have been referred to in the Christian burial service as, "earth to earth, ashes to ashes and dust to dust," are now being resurrected from the ground itself. The passage in the Bible about the Last Judgment speaks about destroying "them which destroy the earth." The Last Judgment can be viewed as "hindsight" evaluation. It is after life has been experienced, and mistakes have been made, that people gain the good judgment that is a trait of those that have lived and erred. They have learned through experience what is important and what is not. Knowing that is the key to good judgment, and is a virtue. It is with these thoughts in mind that I assigned the "Judgment" card as the virtue of the earth element.

The Justice card, especially in medieval Europe, had to do with the death penalty. One could easily lose their life in one of the ancient courts of law by means of a death sentence, which were much more frequent then than in any modern court. The symbols of "justice" were the blindfold, weighing scales and sword. The scales could be easily tipped to one side or the other by the slightest weight. Now, I could say that this card is assigned to the element air because of the scales used in the Egyptian zodiac, but I do not believe Europeans were quite aware of this connection back then. So, going on just the idea of the scales of justice, capable of being tipped by a breeze, and the idea of death as a possible sentence and therefore losing one's life, which can be equated to one's breath or spirit, I assigned this card as the virtue of air.

The Fates

Fire/South	Water/North	Air/West	Earth/East
The Tower	The Lovers	Death	The Wheel

This set of four represents the "uncontrollable forces" around us. The Tower card has also been called "The Lightning Struck Tower" and "The House of God." Today we have a great many buildings that are taller than anything that the ancients could have even imagined. Putting aside building techniques and structural materials that may have been lacking in those old times, there is a little invention, without which even we would not build such tall buildings. That invention: the lightning rod. Building a tower is just asking for lightning to strike at it, that is, unless you build it where there other taller natural objects around it. Then, you lessen the chances of the building being struck, but only somewhat. Lightning strikes were the very the first instances of human beings observing fire being created from where there was no fire before. Fire came from the heavens. God was a thunderbolt hurler, and fire from the heavens is the primary reason there so many of the old Gods that were "thunder Gods," like Zeus, Odin, Thor, Yahweh, and so on.

God was the controller of the natural forces. Storms, tornados, hurricanes, volcanoes were all part of the natural world and completely out of the control of human beings. These were the forces controlled by God and God alone. Fire was the possession of God, and when human beings learned to make fire for themselves, they created myths of a "fire theft" to explain how we got the knowledge away from Him. Therefore, the Tower card represents "the forces of Nature" as uncontrollable by human beings. I associated it with the element fire, because, of the thunderbolt so prominent in the card's image.

"Love is blind." The next card in this set is the "Lovers." What causes someone to love someone? How can love grow for one person when all others see nothing but ugliness? Can we really choose who we love? These are all questions that have yet to be answered adequately. Where the heart wanders is truly "uncontrollable." Even when we view love not just as an emotional response to another person, we are still left with the physical biological need in all creatures to procreate. Procreation is that "attraction" to another that compels us to unite with them and create new life. In addition, we can even consider "love" as the ancient Greeks did. The Greeks had five different words for "love." "Eros" is sexual yearning, desire, or sensual love. "Agape" is love given freely without any thought about the other's worthiness of that love. "Storge" is the love within a family, as the love of parent for child, or brother for brother. "Phile" is the love of "friend for friend." "Epithumia" is love, which is a longing or lust, especially for what is forbidden. When we consider these five types of love, are we really in control when any of them takes hold of us? No. Love also, having been associated for so long with the heart, probably because of the very real pain felt in the chest when we lose someone whom we love, is associated with the vessel of the heart that pumps the blood throughout the body. Therefore, we associate the Lovers card with the element water.

"Death" - the great equalizer. Every one of us will one day face the event of our own demise. We will all die! This is a fact. What can we do about it? Not much. Medical researchers are looking all the time for ways to extend our lives and they have been extended to quite some degree, especially when we compare the average life span today, to say, those of the Middle Ages. There has been some progress and still, we will all die. It's just the way things are. We have no control over death, that's a given, but what happens physically when we die? What did the ancients see about a person's physical body when they died? Well, one moment they were walking around living, breathing, and the next, they're dead. What was the primary way the ancients could tell someone was truly dead? Check the breath, hold a mirror to the person's mouth, to see if there was any hint of breath still there. No breath, no life. Even the word "spirit" means "breath," from the Latin "espiritus." When the spirit leaves the body, the body is dead. Rephrased: "When the breath leaves the body, the body is dead." The two were considered the same thing, as far as the ancients were concerned. Therefore, we assign the Death card to the element air because it is the land of the dead where our "air," or "spirit," goes when the body dies.

The Wheel of Fortune has to do with our physical bodies in several ways. One of these ways, I have already mentioned, is that turn of the wheel and luck of the draw that happens when we are born into this world. Birth is about spirit becoming physical and taking on a body. The circumstances we are born into, is just a spin of the wheel. This is another association we get, by looking at the figures on the wheel itself. We have, around the wheel, what appears to be a youth, a couple of middle-aged people and finally an old man, so the wheel also speaks to the different phases of a human life and how the body ages and eventually dies. Therefore, this card is assigned the element of earth.

Once the elements had been assigned to each of the Trump cards, I could then create a table as follows:

	Fire	Water	Air	Earth
Celestial Spheres	The Sun	The Moon	The Star	The World
Authorities	Emperor	Empress	Priestess	Priest
Fates	The Tower	Lovers	Death	The Wheel
Virtues	Strength	Temperance	Justice	Judgment
Humors	Devil	Hanged Man	Chariot	Hermit

Here were four sets of five cards, one set of five in each of the cardinal directions, that are each assigned to one of the elements. Thinking of the number five, and what type of "five" is commonly associated with each of the directions, led me to thinking about the pentagram that we draw, in ritual, toward each of these directions. Drawing the pentagram, however, is a fairly recent innovation. So, although it's possible to use the pentagram here, it was more likely that the human body with its five appendages was what the originators of the Tarot would have used to represent each set of five cards. This got me to thinking about the propensity the ancients had of relating things to the human body. Certain astrological signs have been assigned to various parts of the body; elements have not only been assigned to particular fingers but functions of the body as well. I started making associations and realized how it was starting to make a lot of sense. These associations could have easily been made with the cards. The head is the "ruler" of the body, the right hand the "hand of control," while the left hand is "uncontrollable," at least for most people; since most people are right-handed. The right leg is the "strongest" of the appendages and is the "foundation" of the body, and finally, the left leg adjusts the "attitude" or "inclination" of the body. With this in mind I made the following attributions: The head was related to the "ruling planets," the right hand related to the "controlling class" or the "authorities," the left hand related to the "uncontrollables" or the "four fates," the right leg was the "foundation" of a human being, related to the "virtues," and the left leg related to the "attitude" or the "four humors."

So, there were six classes of Trump cards, noted in the following table:

	Person	Its Function	The Class
1	Head	Rules the body	Celestial spheres
2	Right hand	Controls physical objects	Authorities
3	Left hand	Uncontrollable; simple grasping	Fates
4	Right leg	Foundation of the body	Virtues
5	Left leg	Adjusts the inclination of the body	Humors
6	The Soul	Learns and experiences life	Fool & Mage

Class six in this table was very interesting to me, because these two cards had been left out of the associations to the body. These two cards represented what inhabits the body; that is, the soul. It is the soul that is born into the body and begins its journey through life. The Fool card has always been said to fit anywhere in the deck; it moves and travels, learning as it goes. The Fool learns, and learns constantly, until one day is recognized as wise and has, by degree, become the Magician. The Fool card is Parzival who wants to be a knight, but knows nothing of knighthood. Eventually Parzival does become a knight, and takes King Arthur's place as king when Arthur dies. He is the Magician in the card that sits at the table with all four suits, represented by tools in front of him. Sitting at that table, he is at the center of the four directions, in the midst of the elements; having achieved a balance between them to make him derive benefits from all of them equally. He is the "juggler" in some decks that manipulates and controls the elements, at his pleasing, and thus impresses all around him by means of his dexterity and cunning. These two cards symbolize the soul, because they are the beginning and end of the journey to wisdom.

So, my discovery of the hidden pattern so far is: four human figures standing in each of the cardinal directions with five cards assigned to each direction and one card, of each set of five, assigned to a single appendage of those human figures. This totals out to twenty cards. At the very center of the four directions sits the Magician, while the Fool walks around the circle, going from one quadrant to the next in his travels to acquire knowledge. It is the ability of the Fool to "travel" from one place to another that also fits in quite nicely with the old teaching about the card, that it can be placed anywhere in the deck. It was like drawing circles with a compass. One point of the compass remains stationary at the center, while the other point traces out the circumference of the circle as it moves around the center. These two points of a compass are represented by the cards of the Magician and Fool. The Magician has found his center and is balanced between the four elements, while the Fool travels, moving from one elemental direction to another, in his search for knowledge. These two additional cards brings the total to twenty-two Trump cards. It was also interesting that I ended the study of the Trump cards as I began it, with a symbol taken from Freemasonry; the compasses.[18]

---

18 *How each of the particular four suit combinations is attributed to an individual card is discuss and analyzed in Appendix 2.*

The Minor Arcana Court Cards

Now to discuss how the Minor Arcana fits into the "secret spread." Please note: I will be dividing the Minor Arcana into two parts and discussing them separately, first the Court Cards and then later the Pip Cards.

The Minor Arcana "Court" cards represent some of the people that you would have seen in the courts of an actual king or queen. All of these cards, when a reading is being done for someone, usually stand for the people that populate a situation. This is the section of the Tarot that is between the higher realm of the deities, or divine forces, represented by the Trump cards and the lower realm, of the primal forces of Nature, represented by the pip cards. In this part of the Tarot deck, we are in the middle ground of the mundane world, and these cards represent the people inhabiting it. Here is where the two great forces of Nature, represented by the number two, are multiplied by themselves four times, the number of the elements, and result in the formulas: $2 \times 2 \times 2 \times 2 = 16$ or $2^4=16$. We will make use of another formula though, as describing this group of cards, which is 4 x 4 = 16. The reason for this is that there are four types of court cards each in one of four suits; the total equaling 16 cards and because the ancients had a very interesting way of posing questions in the form of "either, or" it formed a series of dichotomies. For example, things are either "up" or they are "down"; then, they are either "right" or they are "left." With just these two dichotomies, we arrive at four possible combinations, up-right, up-left, down-right, down-left; 2 x 2 = 4.

To understand the court cards and their relationships to one another, we have to understand how the people of the early Renaissance understood the figures on them. The figures are as follows: king, queen, knight and knave. In some modern decks, the cards have been changed to: king, queen, prince and princess. If we are to learn what the Tarot cards were created for and the lessons they taught, then we will have to go back to the court cards the originators of the deck had in their own decks and not use the modern ones, where innovations have been made for a variety of reasons.

Modern Tarot card readers have taken to interpreting the court cards as indicative of physical characteristics belonging to an individual e.g. tall, dark, red hair, fair complexion, etc. This way of interpreting the cards is actually quite arbitrary, because it depends largely on the colors of the suits if they are transposed into the suits of a modern deck of playing cards. The originators of the Tarot deck, as we can see from our study of the Trump cards, were much more systematic and mathematical in their cosmology, which it seems is what the cards were meant to illustrate. If we are to follow the example set by the Trump cards and make use of a systematic combination of attributes, then we can use these cards to give us more information about a person than just about their appearance, and more about their personality traits. They can tell us about the inner workings of an individual - knowledge, wisdom, likes and dislikes, attitude, and so on. To interpret these cards, I'm reminded of something my grandmother used to tell me: "Everybody wants something. Find out what that is and you will know who they are." That's a simple statement, but it leads one to thinking about what any one person, or group, wants and then later, how they are going about getting it. That's what the court cards will help us figure out about people.

The court cards divide up very easily along the lines delineated by two dichotomies, in which there are two older and two younger figures and also, two overt and two covert figures. The older figures are the Kings and Queens, while the younger figures are the Knights and Knaves. Then, the overt figures are the Kings and Knights, while the covert figures are the Queens and Knaves. The table would look like this:

Table A

	Overt action	Covert action
Mature	Kings	Queens
Young	Knights	Knaves

The descriptive terms in this table would be relative to each other in the following ways: "Mature" would describe someone that is older, more experienced, wiser, set in their ways, and knowledgeable. "Young" would describe someone that is younger, less experienced, more impetuous, open to new methods and ideas but is less knowledgeable, and therefore, seeking to learn. "Overt Action" would describe a person that is more dominant, aggressive and active in a clearly visible way. "Covert Action" would describe a person that is more submissive, passive and active in a more hidden, behind-the-scenes kind of way. The kings and knights would be considered "overt" in their actions because each is active in a way that puts them directly as involved with external forces and events, whereas the queens and knaves can be considered as "covert" in their actions because they are either assistants to, or advisors for, the kings and knights. Their actions happen where an external observer would not necessarily be aware of what they were doing, in any given situation. The queen acts as an advisor to the king and has familial relationships that function as diplomatic and political alliances for her and her husband. The knave, on the other hand, travels with the knight and is not only a companion, someone to talk to, but does all the necessary work so the knight can carry out his duties, by sharpening swords, cleaning armor, grooming the horses, and so on. This is the first set of four in our formula: $(2 \times 2) \times (2 \times 2) = 16$ or $4 \times 4 = 16$.

The second set of four is the suits of the deck. These suits can be related immediately to the elements, cardinal directions, seasons of the year, the humors, among many other groups of four that relate to our physical world. Taking the elements, for example, we can create a table of dichotomies like we did for the court cards thus:

Table B

	Moist	Dry
Cold	Water	Earth
Hot	Air	Fire

So then, the question to discovering what the teaching of the Court Cards is, is a matter of figuring out how these elemental qualities would have been interpreted to reveal something that would be informative about personalities in general, and still relate to the elements. What generalities can be made that will not only give us insight to a particular individual, but fit a system that can be applied to all human beings in a fairly objective way? We will begin by examining the qualities attributed to the elements by the ancient philosophers. Things "cold" tend to be more solid than things described as "hot," so "cold" is denser and "hot" is finer. Let us use the word "tangible" for "cold" and "abstract" for "hot," in other words, "cold" is something you can take hold of, while "hot" cannot be grasped in quite so literal a fashion. In trying to figure out how the qualities "moist" and "dry" were interpreted, we must consider what was inside the body and what was on the outside. The interior of the body is a mass of moisture with all sorts of fluids throughout. Dryness, on the other hand, is what seems to be on the exterior of the body. The skin, hair, fingernails, toenails, may all be considered dry in relation to what is happening on the inside of the body. Replacing the qualities of the elements with our interpretive terms, we get the following table:

Table C

	Interior	Exterior
Tangible	Water	Earth
Abstract	Air	Fire

Now instead of using the elements, let us convert them into the suits of the Tarot like this: water becomes cups, air becomes swords, earth becomes coins, and fire becomes staves. The reasons for these correspondences are fairly straightforward. A cup holds liquids and so that suit relates easily to the element of water. A sword makes the air audible when it slices through the air and can also be said to release the air, or spirit, from a person's body by stabbing it. Coins are made of metal which is a mineral taken from the earth itself, and are used as a physical representation of a specific value. Staves are made of wood, the most common fuel for fire in ancient times, and could be used to fashion a torch. Table C above now looks like this:

Table D

	Interior	Exterior
Tangible	Cups	Coins
Abstract	Swords	Staves

Taking each of the suits now and relating it to its descriptive terms, we have the following:

- Cups (interior, tangible) being what is "felt" on the inside, which are the emotions and dreams that come from the subconscious mind or the psyche.

- Coins (exterior, tangible) being what can be felt on the outside, which are the injuries, labors, movements, material goods and other various things that relate to the body physically.

- Swords (interior, abstract) being the inner non-tangibles like thought, knowledge, wisdom and so on.

- Staves (exterior, abstract) being what the body will do but has not happened yet. These are the goals the body is moving toward but has not realized, the outer non-tangibles.

We now have all the elements in our formula 4 x 4 = 16. Combining the four human figures with the four suits gives us the sixteen personalities represented by the Tarot's Court cards. Each one of the court cards now has four defining characteristics, two from the first table, A, and two from the last table, D. Taking the first letter of each of the qualities in the Tables A and D, we will use them as a shorthand for each, they are: O=overt,   C=covert,   M=mature, Y=younger,   I=interior,   E=exterior,   T=tangible and A=abstract. This is the resulting table:

Table E

	Cups	Coins	Staves	Swords
Queens	CMIT	CMET	CMEA	CMIA
Knaves	CYIT	CYET	CYEA	CYIA
Knights	OYIT	OYET	OYEA	OYIA
Kings	OMIT	OMET	OMEA	OMIA

The Descriptions of the Court Cards or Sixteen Personality Types

Taking each one of the court cards in turn, let us examine how these combinations define a personality. I will give the shorthand for each personality combination right before its description. Also take note of the idea that the interpretation given here, for each personality type, is by no means the only way they can be interpreted. If you use these interpretations as examples, with some imagination you can arrive at your own descriptions of these personalities by using the characteristics from the "Table E" above. Remember, we are not talking about physical characteristics being represented by the cards, so a queen can represent a male and any of the male cards can represent a female as well, since we are using them to symbolize "personality types."

(Side note: I have been teaching this method of analyzing the Court cards for a couple of decades at least, well before I discovered the pattern in the Trump cards, and have only recently come across a very similar system called the "Myers-Briggs Personality Indicator." Both systems have sixteen personality types and an association with mutually exclusive pairs in defining the types; however, the Tarot had its sixteen types in place since the middle 1300's and the Myers-Briggs system was invented in the 1930's. The two systems seem to have arisen independently of one another, however, there is a tie to alchemy through Carl Jung who studied it extensively and was a mentor to Myers and Briggs. Jung writes in his commentary on The Secret of the Golden Flower, "For in medieval alchemy we have the long-sought connecting link between Gnosis and the process of the collective unconscious that can be observed in modern man.[19]" I believe this connection is the reason for the similarity of the two systems.)

Now, we can write an actual description for the traits that each of the "shorthand" letters represent, like this:

C = Prefers to be active behind the scenes, in a manner that is more covert. Does not like to be in the spotlight and is satisfied more with results than with praise.

O = Prefers actions that are direct, aggressive, and ambitious and likes the attention that these bring. Does not mind being in the foreground and will take the role of leader easily.

M = Acts in a mature and sedate way. Is knowledgeable in chosen field of endeavor. Makes prudent choices based on experience and careful observation of any given situation.

Y = Is always learning new things, but sometimes leaps before looking. Likes to try new things and is fairly comfortable with new situations. Tends to be more creative in the area of problem solving.

---

19 Jung, Carl. *Alchemical Studies: Translated by R. F. C. Hull. Princeton University Press, 1983. P. 4.*

T = Likes to work with hands and manipulate physical objects. Is more concerned with practical results than other concerns. Will more often ask the question, "How does it benefit me or mine?" than any other, when faced with making decisions.

A = Tends toward idealism and likes to think about things a lot. A good planner and organizer, is more comfortable with theory and is usually found deciding how something should be done, rather than doing it.

I = Life is more about emotions and inner feelings. Is a great empathizer. Tends to feel emotions more intensely than other people and is very passionate about any endeavor undertaken.

E = Tends to be very simple, direct and plain spoken when moved to say something. It is the surface and how it appears, interacts and relates to others that is important. Things are what they are, and that's it.

We then replace each letter, in every combination, with the phrases and that gives us a description of the personalities for each of the court cards.

Queen of Cups

CMIT = Prefers to be active behind the scenes, in a manner that is more covert. Does not like to be in the spotlight and is satisfied more with results than with praise. Acts in a mature and sedate way. Is knowledgeable in chosen field of endeavor. Makes prudent choices based on experience and careful observation of any given situation. Life is more about emotions and inner feelings. Is a great empathizer. Tends to feel emotions more intensely than other people and is very passionate about any endeavor undertaken. Likes to work with hands and manipulate physical objects. Is more concerned with practical results than other concerns. Will more often ask the question, "How does it benefit me or mine?" than any other, when faced with making decisions.

Queen of Coins

CMET = Prefers to be active behind the scenes, in a manner that is more covert. Does not like to be in the spotlight and is satisfied more with results than with praise. Acts in a mature and sedate way. Is knowledgeable in chosen field of endeavor. Makes prudent choices based on experience and careful observation of any given situation. Tends to be very simple, direct and plain spoken when moved to say something. It is the surface and how it appears, interacts and relates to others that is important. Things are what they are, and that's it. Likes to work with hands and manipulate physical objects. Is more concerned with practical results than other concerns. Will more often ask the question, "How does it benefit me or mine?" than any other, when faced with making decisions.

Queen of Staves

CMEA = Prefers to be active behind the scenes, in a manner that is more covert. Does not like to be in the spotlight and is satisfied more with results than with praise. Acts in a mature and sedate way. Is knowledgeable in chosen field of endeavor. Makes prudent choices based on experience and careful observation of any given situation. Tends to be very simple, direct and plain spoken when moved to say something. It is the surface and how it appears, interacts and relates to others that is important. Things are what they are, and that's it. Tends toward idealism and likes to think about things a lot. A good planner and organizer, is more comfortable with theory and is usually found deciding how something should be done, rather than doing it.

Queen of Swords

CMIA = Prefers to be active behind the scenes, in a manner that is more covert. Does not like to be in the spotlight and is satisfied more with results than with praise. Acts in a mature and sedate way. Is knowledgeable in chosen field of endeavor. Makes prudent choices based on experience and careful observation of any given situation. Life is more about emotions and inner feelings. Is a great empathizer. Tends to feel emotions more intensely than other people and is very passionate about any endeavor undertaken. Tends toward idealism and likes to think about things a lot. A good planner and organizer, is more comfortable with theory and is usually found deciding how something should be done, rather than doing it.

Knave of Cups

CYIT = Prefers to be active behind the scenes, in a manner that is more covert. Does not like to be in the spotlight and is satisfied more with results than with praise. Is always learning new things, but sometimes leaps before looking. Likes to try new things and is fairly comfortable with new situations. Tends to be more creative in the area of problem solving. Life is more about emotions and inner feelings. Is a great empathizer. Tends to feel emotions more intensely than other people and is very passionate about any endeavor undertaken. Likes to work with hands and manipulate physical objects. Is more concerned with practical results than other concerns. Will more often ask the question, "How does it benefit me or mine?" than any other, when faced with making decisions.

Knave of Coins

CYET = Prefers to be active behind the scenes, in a manner that is more covert. Does not like to be in the spotlight and is satisfied more with results than with praise. Is always learning new things, but sometimes leaps before looking. Likes to try new things and is fairly comfortable with new situations. Tends to be more creative in the area of problem solving. Tends to be very simple, direct and plain spoken when moved to say something. It is the surface and how it appears, interacts and relates to others that is important. Things are what they are, and that's it. Likes to work with hands and manipulate physical objects. Is more concerned with practical results than other concerns. Will more often ask the question, "How does it benefit me or mine?" than any other, when faced with making decisions.

Knave of Staves

CYEA = Prefers to be active behind the scenes, in a manner that is more covert. Does not like to be in the spotlight and is satisfied more with results than with praise. Is always learning new things, but sometimes leaps before looking. Likes to try new things and is fairly comfortable with new situations. Tends to be more creative in the area of problem solving. Tends to be very simple, direct and plain spoken when moved to say something. It is the surface and how it appears, interacts and relates to others that is important. Things are what they are, and that's it. Tends toward idealism and likes to think about things a lot. A good planner and organizer, is more comfortable with theory and is usually found deciding how something should be done, rather than doing it.

Knave of Swords

CYIA = Prefers to be active behind the scenes, in a manner that is more covert. Does not like to be in the spotlight and is satisfied more with results than with praise. Is always learning new things, but sometimes leaps before looking. Likes to try new things and is fairly comfortable with new situations. Tends to be more creative in the area of problem solving. Life is more about emotions and inner feelings. Is a great empathizer. Tends to feel emotions more intensely than other people and is very passionate about any endeavor undertaken. Tends toward idealism and likes to think about things a lot. A good planner and organizer, is more comfortable with theory and is usually found deciding how something should be done, rather than doing it.

Knight of Cups

OYIT = Prefers actions that are direct, aggressive, and ambitious and likes the attention that these bring. Does not mind being in the foreground and will take the role of leader easily. Is always learning new things, but sometimes leaps before looking. Likes to try new things and is fairly comfortable with new situations. Tends to be more creative in the area of problem solving. Life is more about emotions and inner feelings. Is a great empathizer. Tends to feel emotions more intensely than other people and is very passionate about any endeavor undertaken. Likes to work with hands and manipulate physical objects. Is more concerned with practical results than other concerns. Will more often ask the question, "How does it benefit me or mine?" than any other, when faced with making decisions.

Knight of Coins

OYET = Prefers actions that are direct, aggressive, and ambitious and likes the attention that these bring. Does not mind being in the foreground and will take the role of leader easily. Is always learning new things, but sometimes leaps before looking. Likes to try new things and is fairly comfortable with new situations. Tends to be more creative in the area of problem solving. Tends to be very simple, direct and plain spoken when moved to say something. It is the surface and how it appears, interacts and relates to others that is important. Things are what they are, and that's it. Likes to work with hands and manipulate physical objects. Is more concerned with practical results than other concerns. Will more often ask the question, "How does it benefit me or mine?" than any other, when faced with making decisions.

Knight of Staves

OYEA = Prefers actions that are direct, aggressive, and ambitious and likes the attention that these bring. Does not mind being in the foreground and will take the role of leader easily. Is always learning new things, but sometimes leaps before looking. Likes to try new things and is fairly comfortable with new situations. Tends to be more creative in the area of problem solving. Tends to be very simple, direct and plain spoken when moved to say something. It is the surface and how it appears, interacts and relates to others that is important. Things are what they are, and that's it. Tends toward idealism and likes to think about things a lot. A good planner and organizer, is more comfortable with theory and is usually found deciding how something should be done, rather than doing it.

Knight of Swords

OYIA = Prefers actions that are direct, aggressive, and ambitious and likes the attention that these bring. Does not mind being in the foreground and will take the role of leader easily. Is always learning new things, but sometimes leaps before looking. Likes to try new things and is fairly comfortable with new situations. Tends to be more creative in the area of problem solving. Life is more about emotions and inner feelings. Is a great empathizer. Tends to feel emotions more intensely than other people and is very passionate about any endeavor undertaken. Tends toward idealism and likes to think about things a lot. A good planner and organizer, is more comfortable with theory and is usually found deciding how something should be done, rather than doing it.

King of Cups

OMIT = Prefers actions that are direct, aggressive, and ambitious and likes the attention that these bring. Does not mind being in the foreground and will take the role of leader easily.

Acts in a mature and sedate way. Is knowledgeable in chosen field of endeavor. Makes prudent choices based on experience and careful observation of any given situation. Life is more about emotions and inner feelings. Is a great empathizer. Tends to feel emotions more intensely than other people and is very passionate about any endeavor undertaken. Likes to work with hands and manipulate physical objects. Is more concerned with practical results than other concerns. Will more often ask the question, "How does it benefit me or mine?" than any other, when faced with making decisions.

King of Coins

OMET = Prefers actions that are direct, aggressive, and ambitious and likes the attention that these bring. Does not mind being in the foreground and will take the role of leader easily. Acts in a mature and sedate way. Is knowledgeable in chosen field of endeavor. Makes prudent choices based on experience and careful observation of any given situation.

Tends to be very simple, direct and plain spoken when moved to say something. It is the surface and how it appears, interacts and relates to others that is important. Things are what they are, and that's it. Likes to work with hands and manipulate physical objects. Is more concerned with practical results than other concerns. Will more often ask the question, "How does it benefit me or mine?" than any other, when faced with making decisions.

King of Staves

OMEA = Prefers actions that are direct, aggressive, and ambitious and likes the attention that these bring. Does not mind being in the foreground and will take the role of leader easily. Acts in a mature and sedate way. Is knowledgeable in chosen field of endeavor. Makes prudent choices based on experience and careful observation of any given situation. Tends to be very simple, direct and plain spoken when moved to say something. It is the surface and how it appears, interacts and relates to others that is important. Things are what they are, and that's it. Tends toward idealism and likes to think about things a lot. A good planner and organizer, is more comfortable with theory and is usually found deciding how something should be done, rather than doing it.

King of Swords

OMIA = Prefers actions that are direct, aggressive, and ambitious and likes the attention that these bring. Does not mind being in the foreground and will take the role of leader easily. Acts in a mature and sedate way. Is knowledgeable in chosen field of endeavor. Makes prudent choices based on experience and careful observation of any given situation. Life is more about emotions and inner feelings. Is a great empathizer. Tends to feel emotions more intensely than other people and is very passionate about any endeavor undertaken. Tends toward idealism and likes to think about things a lot. A good planner and organizer, is more comfortable with theory and is usually found deciding how something should be done, rather than doing it.

Associating a Court Card to a Particular Person

Now that we have the personalities of the court described, the next logical question is, "How do we pair a card with a particular person?" This is done by making a set of "either, or" questions from the dichotomies in the tables above. For example: a person is either "overt" or "covert." If they tend to be more open about their motives, comfortable in dealing with others, do not mind if attention is given to them, and take the more active role in any particular situation, then they would be classified as "overt." On the other hand, if they keep their motives hidden, are uneasy around crowds, do not like to draw attention to themselves and tend to see how a situation plays itself out before acting, then they would be classified as "covert." Phrasing each of the "paired opposites" in an "either, or" styled question, as follows, will tell you which card they are. Here is how I would determine which card fits a particular person, I will use myself as an example:

- Is he overt or covert? The very first thing that comes to my mind is that I act differently in my personal life, than I do as a public speaker in the Craft. This tells me that we can be different cards, or personas, depending on the situation. So, I will find the card that fits me as "Wiccan priest and public speaker." Answer: Overt; therefore I am either a king or a knight.

- Is he mature or young? Although I believe learning is never "done," overall I am fairly experienced. Answer: Mature; therefore I am a "king."

- Is he more comfortable working with tangible or abstract things? Answer: Abstract; therefore I am either fire or air.

- Is he more concerned with inner feelings or external practical results? Remember that air symbolizes inner thoughts and fire represents external goals.

- Answer: External; therefore my suit is "staves."

The card that would best represent me as a teacher and priest in the Wiccan Craft is, the "king of staves." With these four questions then, it is possible to discern which card would represent any particular person in a given situation, or role. Please notice the words, "given situation." In asking the questions, it becomes apparent that the same person can act differently if the situation changes.

So, in reading the cards or just trying to understand a particular person, remember the words of my grandmother, "Everybody wants something." Always ask yourself, "What do they want?" and "What is their way of getting it?" Looking at the court cards descriptions we can also see that not everyone wants things that are tangible. Some want things much more subtle and relating more to their inner life.

The Minor Arcana Pip Cards

The "Pip" cards are those cards with "spots" on them. This is what the word "pip" means; a spot. The spots are the symbols of each of the four suits, which are: a sword, a coin, a stave and a cup. Each card in this section of the Minor Arcana has a number of pips on it from one to ten. These cards relate to the formula: $1 + 2 + 3 + 4 = 10$ and the Pythagorean figure of the tetractis. Taking the sum in this formula and multiplying it by the number of suits gives us the total number of pip cards in the deck, which is $10 \times 4 = 40$.

The tetractis was the most sacred symbol of the Pythagoreans and was said to have within it all the numbers of the universe. It therefore symbolized all the forces of Nature. In comparing this section of the Tarot deck to the other two sections, we find that those other sections are depicted anthropomorphically while this one is not. In the trump section of the Tarot, the cards represent the deities, while in the court cards the figures represented human beings. In the Pip cards, a different thing is happening.

The cards as they were originally drawn have only the representations of the four suits, but no people on them. In modern decks, this has changed because of Arthur Edward Waite. What he did was depict little scenarios on each of the Minor Arcana cards to facilitate reading them in a divination. This may have helped in not having to memorize the cards' meanings, but it also did something else. What this inadvertently did was impose a very specific "flavor" to each of the cards because the scenes could be seen as happy, sad, depressing, industrious, and so forth, because of the picture. This went contrary to what the original cards were meant to represent. The Pip cards were intended to represent those forces in Nature that could not be "humanized," or more accurately, should not be humanized. We can empathize with the deities of the Trump cards; they have human qualities. We are represented as human beings by the Court cards, but what about those forces in Nature that we cannot relate to? What about them? This is where the Pip cards enter the picture.

The Pip cards represent the abstract forces in Nature in which we find no human qualities. These primal forces engendered all that exists. They are beyond our understanding, even though we may try. These cards represent the underworld as the foundation, or framework upon which existence is built. These forces should not be represented as scenes in which there are human beings and their relationships. Because of what they are, they are best represented by numbers. Numbers are abstract and yet have an order about them as the universe has an order. The Pythagoreans believed that everything had at its core a basis in number, and numbers could explain everything.

The tetractis has many symbolic meanings within it. It is made up of four levels with one point on the top level, two points on the second, three points on the third and four points on the final level at the bottom. Looked at from the standpoint of a geometrician, we have the single point representing the monad. The point has only position as its defining quality and it represents "The One Who is Nameless," the

"All" which exists, but not in any physical sense. This is the first level of existence. The two points of the second level each also have positions but now also have something else, a relationship to one another. This relationship can be defined as a distance between the two points, a line. The line has length as a characteristic, but no depth or breadth. As a line it is defined by position and distance between its two end points, these two points representing the ultimate duality of things, the two great forces in Nature we've spoken of as "love" and "strife." Geometrically, however, the line still is a not a physical thing. The third level has three points in it and the third point is the offspring of the first two. It is the soul, but also a deity as the triangle, created by three points, which has in all times represented a divine nature. It can also represent the three levels of existence that are the upper, middle and lower worlds. Three points define a plane, which has position, length and breadth, but no depth, and so, is still described as not physical. This brings us to the final line, the one with four points. The four points now describe a three-dimensional space, into which an object can be placed. This space has position, length, breadth and also depth. This level of the tetractis represents our world, the tangible and very physical world in which we live. So the tetractis represents all of existence, from the ultimate level of being as "one and indivisible" to "our physical world."

The reason this arrangement of ten points in a triangular form was called the "tetractis," is because each of the sides of the triangle consisted of four points. The word itself means "four" in the Greek language. Looked at in this manner, what we have is the four elements represented on each side of the outer triangle by four points. Drawing a line through these nine outer points, we find that a single point is not a part of that triangle. This point is in the center of the tetractis and represents the "One" as the core of the three worlds, which are represented by each of the sides of the triangle. This brings us back to the description I gave earlier of the "secret layout" of the Tarot cards. Remember the "three layer cake" cut into four pieces? The tetractis refers to this arrangement by having each of its three sides "cut" into four.

So, how does one interpret the Pip cards without the "scenes" placed on them by Waite? Easy enough, since the Pythagoreans believed each number had a meaning inherent in it. Here are the "keywords" I use to remember the meanings of each of the numbers:

1 = first impulse

2 = comparison

3 = mediation

4 = manifestation

5 = conflict

6 = harmony

7 = boredom

8 = rejuvenation

9 = fulfillment

10 = completion

Let us now take each one of the numbers in turn and see why a particular meaning was given to it and how they represent a particular "force" or "energy" in Nature. Understanding the reason for each of the keywords will also help you to remember the meanings of each of the pip cards, which I will explain in a short while.

1. The number "one" is the single point. It is like the first spark off a knife and flint that it takes to start a fire. The one is the very first impulse that gets something moving or growing. It is the first bit of "energy" that is hardly noticeable and yet starts an entire process that may take on enormous proportions. The keywords to remember when you see a "one" card in a reading, no matter the suit, is "first impulse." It can be described as that "outside force" that changes the direction of inertia of any given object and starts it in a new direction; it is the seed that grows an entire tree. It is initiation.

2. The number "two" is two points that have some sort of relationship to one another. Once you introduce a second point, it invites a comparison to the first. This, of course, is true for anything. When you have one of anything,

you simply examine it for what it is. When a second example of the same object is introduced, you now begin to make comparisons; are the objects exactly the same, what differences do they have if any, how close are they to one another, is one better than the other in some way, what is their relationship. Therefore, the key word to remember when you see a "two" card is "comparison."

3. The number "three" introduces a third point. Once we examine more than one point, it is always about the relationship between the points. In the case of a third point, it is about its position in relation to the first two points. Is the third point closer to one point or the other? Is it equal distance? The third point "mediates" or defines the space between the first two points and can be said to "favor" one side or the other by its proximity to one of the points, or not favor either by being exactly halfway between them. So, the third point's keyword to remember is "mediation."

4. The number "four" brings us to the number so important in the Tarot system. It

relates to the four directions, four seasons, four elements and that level in the tetractis that geometrically defines a "space" into which a physical object can be placed. It is the first introduction of "physicality" which the first three points lacked, so this number represents "manifestation," the first noticeably physical effects of the flow of energy that began at the number one. The keyword for the number four is "manifestation."

5. The number "five" is the first number that is beyond the four levels in the tetractis, and it begins to combine two of the previous numbers into one. Five combines the numbers "two" and "three" and so also combines their meanings. Two is a comparison and three is about mediation. In five, we have just past the experience of manifestation in "four" and are in that state of making comparisons between where we were, before the physical event, and where we are now. It is as if we had an idea or plan, prior to the physical occurrence, and then, the actual manifestation happens. Now, we are in the state immediately afterward. The

comparison is between these two, how the event may or may not match the original idea or theory, is what "five" is all about. This number is about "theory versus practice" and how these sometimes diverge. When a theory is put into practice, there are always some differences between what we thought was going to occur and what actually occurs. This produces dissatisfaction. This is not a bad dissatisfaction, but the kind necessary to begin making adjustments, either in the theory or the application, so we can arrive at the point of mediation between the two. The keyword for this number is "conflict," between what was and what should be; between theory and practice.

6. The number six is the solution for the problem in number five. In "five," theory and practice were in discord and it presented problems. We talked about having to make adjustments, either to the theory, the practice, or both. In the number six, what we have is an adjustment to the two by using two "threes" to make the six. Remember three's keyword was "mediation" which is an adjustment, or

compromise, of some kind. In "six" we have made two adjustments; one to the idea, ideal or theory, and the other to the practice, implementation, and/or physical application of that ideal. We have brought the two realms of abstract and tangible into harmony in this number. The keyword for the number "six" is "harmony."

7. As you may have noticed, each of the numbers incorporates the number before it, in the natural counting sequence, and then adds to it by making a slight change in meaning. The number "seven" has prior to it the very good number of "six." However, as with anything else, you can still get too much of a "good thing," even harmony. What would it mean to have too much harmony? Well, it would bring on stagnation and boredom. Without something to struggle with, work for, or against, we grow complacent and movement toward greater levels of achievement is halted. We become bored. Interestingly, this number is equated to a marital difficulty called the "seven year itch." It's not that things aren't going well, it's that they have

been going "too well" for too long and the mind begins to look for things that are "entertaining." The keyword for "seven" is "boredom."

8. "Eight" is the solution for the number "seven." In "eight" we have two "fours." Remember "four" was "manifestation," which is something physically making an appearance in your environment. When something is new, it creates excitement and definitely, interest. The only way to move past the boredom of "seven" is to revitalize that excitement you felt when experiencing that first something new in your world. The way to do that is, either do the old thing in a new way, or find a new thing to do that gives you a new focus and excitement as the old thing did before. "Eight" is two "fours" the second "four" being the revitalization of the experience felt with the first "four." The keyword for the number "eight" is "rejuvenation."

9. "Nine" is three "threes." Three was the number of "mediation" and now we find this "three" making its appearance in three different places. The first place was in the abstract realm

of the mind, as an idea or theory. The second place was when it manifested in the physical world, as something practical. The third place is now the realm of the spirit. We have now moved the experience into the place of spiritual fulfillment. The balancing of two forces into a third is now taking place in three places at once, in the mind, the body and the spirit. "Nine" is about being fulfilled at all levels of being; body, mind and soul. The keyword for the number "nine" is "fulfillment."

10. "Ten" is the number of completion. All that can be done on this particular path that has been followed to this point, and is now finished. All the benefit that can be derived, has been. It is done. It is time to start something totally new and unrelated. The keyword for the number "ten" is "completion."

I will now summarize all the numbers as a series of events in a process, so that you can get a general overview of their meanings. Summation: "One, an idea sparks your interest. Two, you compare it to a second idea. Three, you make a choice and/or adaptation. Four, you implement that choice. Five, the practical application doesn't match the theoretical idea. Six, you make adaptations and things go well. Seven, you get bored with the sameness. Eight, you find a way to revitalize your enthusiasm. Nine, the work now fulfills you in mind, body and soul. Ten, it is finished."

To get the meanings of all forty pip cards we create a table, much like we did for the Court cards, but this time we place each of the numbers 1 through 10 in each suit and combine the keyword for each number with the meanings already given to the suits in the last section about the Court cards.

	Staves	Cups	Swords	Coins
1	New direction	Attraction	Inspiration	Accident
2	Fork in the road	Second thoughts	Analysis	Choice
3	Path chosen	Courtship	Theory	Adapt-ation
4	Journey begun	Requited	Experiment	Acqui-sition

	Staves	Cups	Swords	Coins
5	Obstacles	Annoy-ances	Contrary data	Malfunc-tion
6	Clearly mapped	Love	Discovery	Func-tioning
7	White line hypnosis	Wandering eyes	Stagnation	Rote action
8	Second wind	Marriage	New information	New method
9	Finding your zone	Settling in	Proof	Mastery
10	Journey ended	Family	Implement-ation	Tradition

Table of keywords for the forty Pip cards.

It should be remembered that the keywords in this table, for each card, are not the only ones that can be used. The best thing to do is remember the meanings for the individual numbers and suits. Then, you can blend these meanings for each reading, or situation, at any given moment. Doing this will give you a keyword more appropriate for that instant and will not be quite so limiting as to any particular card's meaning. Practicing making a table like the one above is also a valuable exercise and should be done without referencing anything except your own inspiration.

Understanding Groups of Tarot Cards according to their Relationships

Now we come to trying and understand what the creators of the Tarot system were trying to teach. Figuring this out is the hardest part of deciphering the Tarot system. We do have a lot of material from the ancient Pagan philosophers still available, but not all and definitely not the secret material given only to initiates of the old mystery traditions. We have the system of the Tarot laid out and its pattern explained; however, it is more of an outline, or series of pictorial notes, than a precise explanation of those old Pagan teachings. Maybe, this is the way it was intended to be. As it is, with an understanding of the secret pattern, we can now use its structure to organize and try to understand what those ancient teachers have left us in written form. In this section we will derive meaning from the cards themselves. I will give some references to some of the still existing material, written by the ancient philosophers, that has some connection to the Tarot's symbolism. What I will do is give you a start on studying the Tarot teachings for yourself, by pointing out the different card groupings and the most obvious relationships between individual cards. A word of warning: the Tarot is subject to many interpretations, and the meanings I see in the cards are not the only ones possible. Therefore, take my ideas about these relationships as suggestions for further inquiry and study.

As can be seen by looking at the "secret layout" of the cards, the cards can be grouped in a variety of ways according to what category one is focusing on. We can make some logical guesses about what would have been included as topics for study associated with the Tarot just by looking at the way the cards relate to one another. Here is a list of the various groupings of the cards possible in the layout:

- **Cards by "levels of being."** The Trump Cards: the deities, the Court Cards: people that make up our society, and the Pip Cards: the primal forces of Nature.

- **Cards by "element."** Staves: fire, Cups: water, Swords: air, and Coins: earth.

- **Cards by "category."** The head: the celestial spheres, the right hand: the authorities, the left hand: the fates, the right leg: the virtues, the left leg: the humors, and the two soul cards: the Fool and Mage.

As we look at the different groups, you will notice that individual cards may be talked about more than once or even twice. This is because many cards are associated with more than one group, because of overlapping meanings. For example: the Emperor card can be talked about as a "fire card," a "ruler card," or a "deity card." So, just as people have different types of relationships in their lives, so too the cards have different relationships to other cards. Let's now look at each of these groups and see what may have been taught about them in the past.

The Three Levels of Existence

A very simple way of locating one's self in any situation, is to see wherever we are, as "here." This may seem very obvious, but it starts to make more sense when you see "here" in relation to "where we've been" and to "where we're going." This relationship then points to our location in terms of a journey. This journey can then be seen as a journey of "evolution" or, of "growth," or "progress" towards a goal. Depending on what we wish to focus, the "here" changes accordingly. Viewing the past, or where we've been, as something that can no longer be changed, we must then use what we've learned from it, and use it as a tool we now have available to us, for the manipulation of the future. The very best way to foretell the future, after all, is to make it. This is viewing the "here" in a "horizontal" sense. The "here" can also be viewed with a "vertical" perspective. Seeing "here" in terms of spirituality, we can relate our "here" to being between the primal forces of Nature that are beneath us and serve as the foundation for the cosmos, and what is above us, which are the deities that control these forces. If we take as a lesson the previous perspective of a "journey," then we know that we are constantly moving the "here" from the past toward the "here" in the future. So, this tells us that "vertically" we are also moving our "situation" from being "primal" toward becoming "deities." That is, beings that are more and more in control of the forces of nature within ourselves.

This triplicity also speaks to us of the triune nature of the Supreme Being; the One which is All. The words often equated with the Supreme Being are "was, is and always will be." These words not only show the deity as having three aspects, but also that, with respect to the One, everything exists within the One, whether it be in the past, present or future and we live within those three levels of existence. "The trinity of the deity, in one mode or other, has been article in all creeds. It creates, preserves, and destroys. It is the generative power, the productive capacity, and the result.[20]"

So, what do we learn from the three levels of the Tarot? We learn that wherever, or whoever, we are, we are moving from one state of being to another constantly. We also learn that we can control, to a greater or lesser degree, our

---

20 Pike, Albert. *Morals and Dogma of the Ancient and Accepted Scottish Rite of Freemasonry Prepared for the Supreme Council of the Thirty-third Degree, for the Southern Jurisdiction of the United States, and Published By Its Authority. Charleston Southern Jurisdiction, 1919. P. 57.*

situation depending on how well we learn from our past, make use of the tools we have in the present, and use what we have to "make" our future.

The Trump Cards (The Deities)

The deities are the forces of nature in human form. These forces were represented previously by the Pip Cards and the tetractis, however, in that form they are much too abstract for an individual to be able to relate to them. As the Trump cards and the deities, we can now relate and empathize with these forces. In them, we find that these forces are a part of us and not only move within us, but also compel us to action. It is through the deities that we can understand the forces of Nature as also being within each one of us. It has been said, "If God did not exist we would need to create him." Well, the same can be said of all the Gods and Goddesses; if they did not exist, then we would need to create them. This is because somehow we, as human beings, must come to an understanding of our place in the grand scheme of things. But human beings are more than just logic and reason, we are also "heart and soul." "Because there are innumerable things beyond the range of human understanding, we constantly use symbolic terms to represent concepts that we cannot define or fully comprehend. This is one reason why all religions employ symbolic language or images. But this conscious use of symbols is only one aspect of a psychological fact of great importance; Man also produces symbols unconsciously and spontaneously, in the form of dreams.[21]" It is through subconscious connection that the Tarot gives us its greatest benefit. It talks to us in the language of dreams, it helps us by giving us a structure and format in which we can connect to in a logical and reasonable way, while also linking this structure to images that we connect to emotionally, and so, also have a symbolic method for understanding the cosmos. This is why we have books of poetry, instead of just dictionaries. The deities, because of their personalities, allow us to

---

21 Jung, Carl G. *Man and His Symbols*. *Dell Publishing Co., Inc.* 1968. P. 4.

connect to them at levels of awareness that are not only conscious but subconscious and intuitive. They are the way we are "hooked into" the cosmos around us and so, through them, we can understand, adapt to, and maybe even, control forces that are normally beyond our small domain.

The Court Cards (Society)

The Court Cards are the cards that represent people, and there is one common thing that can be said about people all over the world: "Everyone wants something." That being said, we can further deduce that everyone must have a certain "way" or "style" for getting what they want. The Court Cards represent the different ways and styles that these people go about getting what they want. They also represent their different levels of experience and knowledge, what their main areas of interest are, and how they interact with others.

The Pip Cards (The Primal Forces of Nature)

The "lowest" of these three levels is that of the "primal forces of Nature." This is the level represented by the pip cards, being four groups of ten cards. The Pythagoreans considered the number ten as the most sacred number, being the source of all things and having all things within it. The power of Nature is immense and impersonal. This is represented by the pure abstract nature of number in the Tetractis. As human beings, we try to understand Nature to the best of our abilities and, in so doing, we notice that number is the language of existence. This is the reason our sciences so often describe Nature by the use of mathematics. Many modern decks have changed the pip cards so they have on them pictures of people engaged in a variety of activities. This is not so in the oldest forms of the Tarot. The pip cards were intended to point to those forces of Nature that are impersonal, as opposed to the forces in Nature that have been "personalized" in the Trump cards. These two parts of the deck are important each in their own way, because they illustrate the powers of Nature in two very different manners. The Tarot gives us a lesson about Nature by telling us that looked at in one way, the way of the Trump cards, it seems we can understand it and relate to it. Then again, looked at in another way, the way of the pip cards, it is cold and indifferent to our status in life. "Nature does not act from any wish to be benevolent; it deals with all things as poppets of grass used in magical rites.[22]"

It is difficult to understand that in Nature; great destruction, pain, and death are simply part of the natural course of events. We often ask why there is "evil" in the world, but we never ask, "Why do we need to subtract or divide in mathematics? Aren't we hurting the original number by diminishing it?" No, we don't ask that. Because numbers are impersonal, just as the forces of Nature are impersonal and have no special preference for any of the creatures in it; the benefit of one, to the detriment of another, is simply part of the larger equation. Nothing personal.

---

22 Wolfsong, Boniface. *The Wiccan Way: A Reinterpretation of the Tao Te Ching.* The Lycian Sanctuary. 2013. P. 23.

The Suits (The Elements)

The elements are the building blocks of the universe, but can also be symbolic of the building blocks of our society. They are also the foundation for the structure of the Tarot deck, as everything within the deck is adapted to, and from, the number of suits and elements, which is four. The suits in the pip cards are the basic forces, of Nature, that are the foundation of our world. The elements combine in various ways to create all the forms that exist in the material world. The suits in the court cards represent different fields of interest or action. One series of attributions to the suits, related to social structure, are: swords representing the military class, coins representing the mercantile class, cups representing the clergy and scholarly class, and finally, the staves representing the government or governing class, royalty, politicians, and so on. Then, there are the Trump cards that represent the deities and are associated with the elements as well. These are the personalities that help us to connect with and understand the grand forces of Nature.

The Stave Cards (The Fire Element)

Fire has the qualities of being "hot" and "dry." Fire is active and destructive, as it consumes whatever it comes into contact with. It seems very much like a living creature in that it, 1) reproduces others like itself without diminishing the original, 2) "feeds" off its environment by taking in "energy," 3) avoids decay in itself by causing decay in its environment, and 4) it gives off heat as a result of its metabolic chemical processes. Personally, I consider fire to be a form of life, although one very alien to what we normally regard as a living being.

Because fire is continually moving and consuming; we can relate this to our lives. We continually move and seek to accomplish certain goals. Therefore, the staves represent our will, or the will to do, to take control, to accomplish, to take charge, to manage, and ultimately consume.

The Cup Cards (The Water Element)

Water has the qualities of being "cold" and "moist." Water is passive, in that it must be "acted upon" in order for it to have any motion.

Water is moved by gravity, wind, earthquakes; however, if left to its own devices water will simply rest. Water has a reflective surface, which means that when we look at a body of water, we tend to see only its surface and what is beneath that is hidden from view. This is symbolic of our inner life, emotions, and psyche, all of which are hidden within us, beneath a superficial exterior. This also relates to the relationships in our lives and how they affect our inner sense of well-being.

The Sword Cards (The Air Element)

Air has the qualities of being "hot" and "moist." Air is active and life-sustaining, and in fact represents life itself in western culture by being the "spirit" which is the "breath." Without the air we breathe we would all expire, obviously. So many of our words speak of this quality of air as the "life-force" itself. It also represents our thoughts and ability to reason. Although we are all aware of our thoughts, there is really nothing physical which can grasp and say, "these are my thoughts." Those things of the mind, ideas, logic, reasoning ability, planning, and so forth, are all related to the element of air as they are intangible, yet very real, just like the spirit.

The Coin Cards (The Earth Element)

Earth has the qualities of being "cold" and "dry." Earth is passive, except for earthquakes, and remains at rest. It is our foundation. It is the ground we stand on and represents the principles we live by as landmarks that guide us in our journey through life. It also represents our physicality. We have a body, and its limitations and abilities are those things which we must consider when making decisions. The practical application of forces under our control must be applied in a manner that is in keeping with having a physical body. The body is the earthy part of ourselves and returns to earth when we die. It is us in solid form, living in this physical world.

The Planet Cards (The Head)

These are the "celestial spheres," and we know them by the planets in each one. The planet cards are assigned to the head. It is the head that sets the agenda for the rest of the body. The "music" of these celestial spheres is the background and influence for everything we do in our lives. It is the matrix, or ground, of our being.

The Authority Cards (The Right Hand)

The right hand is, for most people, the hand that controls things. It manipulates and is the hand does the work that requires skill and finesse. Here is where we locate the Authority cards. These are the cards that represent the authorities in our lives. To a certain extent, they control us. The Tarot splits these authorities in a couple of different ways. First, it splits the secular from the spiritual worlds, and each of these worlds has its own authority figures. The Emperor and Empress are the secular figures, and the Priest and Priestess are the spiritual.

It also splits these four cards by gender. The Emperor and Priest are male figures, and the Empress and Priestess are female. So, not only are the different authorities active in different areas of social interest, they also have different ways of dealing with the situations that arise in each. The male figures tending to be more overt and aggressive, while the female figures are softer and more diplomatic.

The Fate Cards (The Left Hand)

The left hand is the "uncontrollable" hand, in that most people are right-handed and exercise very little control over the left. It represents those things in life that we have very little control over, like the circumstances of our birth, the weather, who we will fall in love with, and how we will die. These things are for fate to decide. In some of the oldest cards, figures in these cards had on blindfolds. This was to show how we could not foresee the effects, or outcomes, of these forces at work in our lives.

The Virtue Cards (The Right Leg)

What is a virtue? The word "virtue" comes from the Latin "virtus," which equated to "manliness." In other words, a virtue is what separated the men from the boys, guidelines and boundaries as to what a person would and wouldn't do in their daily lives that made them honorable, or not. The virtue cards in the Tarot are four and each one relates to a different aspect of one's life. Each of us can act in a variety of ways depending on the situation. For example, a person may never consider stealing from a friend, but wouldn't even give it a second thought when stealing a company pen from work. The difference here being that in the first case a known individual is hurt, and in the second, only a vague and unknown conglomeration of entities collectively known as "the company." Now, a different person would not consider the party hurt; others would only consider the act itself as being hurtful. It is the very act of stealing that is wrong for this kind of person and they would not do the act, no matter who the victim is. So what defines a virtue? Virtue "contains three elements: reason, power, and deliberate choice. The soul's reasoning power's virtue is wisdom, which is a habit of contemplating and judging. The irascible part's virtue is courage, which is a habit of enduring dreadful things, and resisting them. The appetitive part's of virtue is temperance, which is a moderation and detention of the pleasures which arise from the body. The whole soul's virtue is justice, for men indeed become bad either through vice, or through incontinence, or through a natural ferocity.[23]" The four cards in the Tarot that represent the virtues are as follows: the "Judgement" card represents wisdom, the "Strength" card is symbolic of courage, the "Temperance" card represents the reasoned control of the body's appetites, and the "Justice" card represents the virtue of giving everyone and everything according to their just due.

The Humor Cards (The Left Leg)

The humor cards relate to what the ancients called the four fluids, also called "the humors," within the human body. Depending on the predominance of one or more of the humors and their mixture, the temperament of the person was said to be affected. This brings to mind the "four temperaments" or "personality types"

---

23 *Guthrie, Kenneth S. The Pythagorean Sourcebook and Library. Phanes Press, Grand Rapids, Michigan, USA 1987. P. 225.*

related to the humors, which were: melancholic, phlegmatic, sanguine, and choleric.

The Fool and Mage Cards (The Soul)

The cards representing the soul are the Fool and Mage. The two cards are polar opposites of one another: one is foolish, ignorant, naive, and seen traveling or wandering about, while the other is wise, cunning, knowledgeable and seen as stationary, because of his position behind a "work table" or "altar." The Fool depicted in the Visconti-Sforza tarot is holding a stick or club. This relates easily to the suit in the deck of staves. Remember the staves represent the element fire and have to do with the will. The Mage, on the other hand, has before him all four elements represented by coins, a cup, a knife and he is holding a wand, which can be seen as a more sophisticated version of the Fool's club. This would seem to be indicating that the Fool only possesses a "will" or a desire for things or want to go places, whereas the Mage is in possession, and control of, not only the "desire," but the knowledge, material means and emotional maturity to do what is necessary in life. The Mage is also seated or standing behind a table, which means he is firm on his ground, and recalls the position of the Buddha in his "ground touching pose." The Buddha, after his enlightenment, was challenge one final time by the "great tempter" Mara, who told the Buddha that since he had now transcended the material world that he should leave it, but the Buddha, instead touched the ground and thereby, in essence, said, "I know my own mind and here I will remain." This is the Mage of the Tarot, confident and knowledgeable in who he is as a result of his life experience and wisdom gained through having been the "fool" and traveling the world until he finally reaches that still spot at the center of every circle.

The Complementary Trump Cards

"To know beauty is to give birth to ugliness. To be aware of virtue also means to acknowledge where it is absent. So it is, that being and non-being produce one another; the difficult and the easy give meaning one another." - Lao Tzu

It was very obvious to me, by this point, that the Tarot was based on a long series of dichotomies. So, just as an experiment, I took the elemental combinations that I had arrived at earlier for each card, and then changed each element in the combination to its opposite. Thinking about the qualities of each of the elements, you see that "dry" is opposed to "moist," and "cold" is opposed to "hot." So theoretically, when "hot" and "cold" are paired, their combined value is "null." In other words, the forces represented by each quality are perfectly balanced when related to its opposite. Extending this logic to the elements, fire is opposed to water because each has qualities that are balanced by its opposite element. Changing an elemental combination, by changing every one of its components to its opposite, I then read that combination to find the two trump cards that could be said to "balance each other out." In the descriptions of the Trump cards below, I have given each card's "paired opposite" as its "complementary card." Comparing any "balanced pair," we can now see the relationship between the two cards that gives more information about the specific attributes of each card that the originators of the Tarot would have been referring to. It tells us for example, that the "Wheel of Fate," when paired with the "Death" card as its opposite, is not so much about what fate has in store for you in the future, but instead what fate had in store for you at your birth, birth being the opposite of death. The card, then, would be about the circumstances of your birth and the seeming randomness of that event, and not your eventual fate. This means that the fate spoken of in the Tarot is like the luck you have when playing cards. No one can say what cards you will be dealt at the time of your birth.

What I will do now is discuss the trump cards, but instead of taking them in the order that is normally given in most books on the Tarot, I will pair them up with their complementary cards. Since the original cards didn't have numbers on them to begin with, it shouldn't change the meanings of the cards in anyway to interpret them in a different order than the one they are normally given in other books.

The Fool and Mage (complementary cards)

Alternate Titles	Le Fou Le Mat	The Magus The Magician The Juggler Le Bateleur
Card's Group	soul	soul
Placement	traveling the perimeter of the circle	the center of the circle
Associated Element	earth	air
Body Appendage	none	none
Element Combination	South = coins North = swords West = cups East = staves	South = swords North = coins West = staves East = cups

Ignorance - Knowledge (The Soul's Journey)

The Mage and Fool cards are about knowledge and ignorance. In speaking of a human life, we start out naive and ignorant of what awaits. Yet, we are full of energy and ready to face whatever comes. The Fool carries a traveler's bag, and this symbolizes that he is in constant motion. At the other end of the spectrum is a person who has lived, learned, and is very knowledgeable, but has become sedentary and centered in his own being. No longer moving, the Mage is waiting for others to come to him, to his table. This person has the wisdom gained through experience. It is this wisdom that people seek when they come to him. So, the two ends of the spectrum are the Fool, the naive ignorant soul just beginning life, and the Mage, who has the experience of having lived and learned, and now informs others.

The ideas of movement and stillness are very important symbols in these two cards. Someone who is young has a lot of energy and will normally move quite a lot, whereas someone who is older and has become more stable, is able to center themselves in the knowledge of who they are. It has been stated many times, in various books on the Tarot, that the Fool can be placed anywhere in the deck and has no clearly assigned number or place. This shows its "moveable" nature. The Mage, on the other hand, either stands or sits before a table, with his tools laid out before him, motionless. He is centered.

The Star and the World (complementary cards)

Alternate Titles	L'etoille	Le Monde
Card's Group	Celestial spheres	Celestial spheres
Placement	In the west	In the east
Associated Element	Air	Earth
Body Appendage	Head	Head
Element Combination	South = swords North = coins West = cups East = staves	South = coins North = swords West = staves East = cups

Spirit - Matter (heaven and earth)

The Star card is a very interesting card. It can be seen as one of the more complex cards in the Tarot deck, mythologically speaking. As we have already seen, the star shown on the card refers to the planet Venus. The planet Venus was also known as the Morning and Evening Star, and fell from being the former to becoming the latter. It was also known as Lucifer in Roman times, which means that it brought light, or knowledge, and its time of day was at twilight.

The card's direction is the West, which is the place of death, and we have depicted on the card a woman pouring water from two jugs into a river. This is very likely a reference to the "Styx Oath." Because the Goddess Styx was the first to side with Zeus in the war with the Titans, he rewarded her by causing all the deities to be bound by her. The river Styx is the "fence" or boundary that separates the material world from the world of the spirit.

The World card is the physical world, composed of the four elements, divided into four seasons, between the four directions, and so on. So, in these two cards we have the two worlds of spirit and matter illustrated. Each of these worlds is kept separate by the river Styx.

———

The Moon and The Sun (complementary cards)

Alternate Titles	Le Lune	El Sol
Card's Group	Celestial spheres	Celestial spheres
Placement	In the north	In the south
Associated Element	Water	Fire
Body Appendage	Head	Head
Element Combination	South = cups North = staves West = swords East = coins	South = staves North = cups West = coins East = swords

Obscure - Apparent (subjective & objective)

The Sun and Moon cards point out the difference between seeing things in the bright clear light of day or under the dim light of the moon, when it's darker and more obscure.

We wake up in the morning, get out of bed and prepare ourselves for the day. We move out into the world and it is brightly lit; we look at people, we talk to them, we work, we play, and everything is as it seems. This is the world of our everyday conscious selves. This is the world of the Sun card. Things are what they are.

In contrast to this, as we move toward the twilight of the day, the sun sets and we find that things are being obscured, the light is dimmer, and we can't quite see things as clearly as we did just hours earlier. We prepare ourselves for sleep, we go to bed and we dream. We have now entered the world of mystery and illusion. Not only are things not clear, but in our dreams things change, often from one thing to another, without us even knowing why. Our dreams use a language of symbols. Symbols can have one meaning, or many, at different levels of understanding. Not only that, we don't know, at times, what all of these meanings could be, or how to interpret them. So, we are left guessing. It's a mystery. This is the world of the Moon card.

———————————

The Priestess and Priest (complementary cards)

Alternate Titles	The High Priestess La Papesse	The High Priest The Pope The Hierophant Le Pape
Card's Group	Authorities	Authorities
Placement	In the west	In the east
Associated Element	air	Earth
Body Appendage	Right hand	Right hand
Element Combination	South = swords North = cups West = coins East = staves	South = coins North = staves West = swords East = cups

Esoteric - Exoteric (Spiritual Authorities)

The Priest and Priestess represent a dichotomy that occurs in every religion. All religious rituals have two parts to them. There is the outer part, which believers are instructed to perform in order to recognize a particular event, and they do it because they have been taught to do it, maybe since childhood, as an outward sign of belief in the tenets of the religion. This is the ritual as simple rote form.

Then there is the other part, the inner lessons that come with understanding the spirituality behind the form of the ritual. This is understanding the "why" behind a ritual's symbolic actions; the esoteric meaning behind the actions, symbols, and tools, used in the performance of the ritual.

The Priest represents the exoteric part of a religion, which are the ritualized observances, and the Priestess represents the esoteric portion, which is the spirituality at the core of every religion, that gives it meaning. Notice the positions of the hands in the two cards. In the Priest card, he is performing a blessing. He is looking outward, either at the viewer of the card, or toward the viewer plus others depicted on the card itself, as a group that stands in front of him receiving his blessing. In the Priestess card, she is either holding a book, or pointing to a book; there is no one standing in front of her. The book symbolizes study, but which also involves meditation, contemplation, and prayer. All of these things being done alone, as the Priestess is alone, and unattached. The book represents a personal knowledge of the teachings at the core of any religion; a personal gnosis.

The Emperor and Empress (complementary cards)

Alternate Titles		
Card's Group	Authorities	Authorities
Placement	In the north	In the south
Associated Element	Water	Fire
Body Appendage	Right hand	Right hand
Element Combination	South = cups North = swords West = staves East = coins	South = staves North = coins West = cups East = swords

War - Peace (Secular Authorities)

The difference between the Emperor and the Empress is as vast as that between war and peace. On the one hand, you have the Emperor, who is about dominating, conquering, fighting, and even killing, in order to acquire new lands to create an empire. The Empress, on the other hand, is normally depicted as pregnant. As a pregnant woman she gives life, she nurtures, she nests. She is at home.

In order for the Emperor to perform his function, he must wander from home, he must go out and search for new territories to make his own. His function is to move, to conquer; this is what the Emperor is about doing. He is like a fire that is continually consuming its surroundings, and fire is the element he is associated with.

The Empress is associated with the water element. Water is necessary for life, she nurtures others, she fosters their growth, she makes them live. This is the exact the opposite of what the Emperor does. She is life nurturing.

———

The Lovers and The Tower (complementary cards)

Alternate Titles	L'amoureux	Lightning Struck Tower The House of God La Maison Dieu
Card's Group	Fates	Fates
Placement	In the north	In the south
Associated Element	Water	Fire
Body Appendage	Left hand	Left hand
Element Combination	South = cups North = swords West = coins East = staves	South = staves North = coins West = swords East = cups

Unifying - Separating

In Nature, things are always in motion. Because things are constantly moving, they are either moving towards one another, or away from one another. In alchemy the words used to describe these movements are "coagula et solve," in English, "coagulating and dissolving."

The Lovers card symbolizes those forces in Nature which unify, that blend things together to become one. It can also symbolize gravity. Gravity is the tendency of two masses to pull towards one another. Then there is magnetism; this again is the tendency of things to pull toward one another. The Lovers card represents the "law of attraction" in Nature.

The Tower card represents repulsion. In physics, this is the tendency of particles, or bodies with the same electrical charge, or magnetic polarity, to repel one another. It also speaks to the "law of thermal expansion." This is the tendency of things to expand when they are heated. When expansion is at work, and we try to keep things together by confining the expansion, it will continue to the point that an explosion will occur. This is the ultimate act of repulsion.

In the grand scheme of things, what we have in the Lovers and Tower cards are the Big Bang, which is the first primal expansion, in contrast to the big crunch, which is all things pulling back together to form an ultimate unity.

———————————

The Wheel and Death (complementary cards)

Alternate Titles	The Wheel of Fate The Wheel of Fortune	La Mort
Card's Group	Fates	Fates
Placement	In the east	In the west
Associated Element	Earth	Air
Body Appendage	Left leg	Left hand
Element Combination	South = coins North = staves West = cups East = swords	South = swords North = cups West = staves East = coins

Birth - Death

The attributes of the Wheel of Fortune card places it in the east, the quadrant of birth or new life. The fact that it has illustrated on it a roulette type of wheel tells us that it involves chance and those things random about being born, like the circumstances into which one is born, e.g. parents, country, economic status, and so on. The Goddess possibly being referenced is the Roman Goddess Fortuna, as we can read in the following passage from the book A History of Pagan Europe, "Servius Tullius was also credited with building the temple of Fortuna, who became notorious in Imperial times as the goddess of blind chance. She was, however, originally a goddess of plenty, ruling childbirth and later the fate of children. Fortuna had an oracle at Praeneste, which operated not through seership but through the drawing of lots. It is easy to see how, once her agricultural roots were forgotten, she could develop into the goddess of blind fate which she later became.[24]" So the card speaks to us of our births and how they are much like a game of chance, in which the spin of the wheel or the cards dealt are random, and what makes a real difference is how we as individuals choose to play the game. The pure "luck of the draw" is even exhibited by the blindfold over the eyes of the female on the card,

---

24 Jones, Prudence and Pennick, Nigel. A History of Pagan Europe. Routledge, London and New York, 1995. P. 39.

who represents the Goddess, depicted at the center of the wheel.

━━━━━━━━━━━━━━━

Strength and Temperance (complementary cards)

Alternate Titles	Fortitude La Force	
Card's Group	Virtues	Virtues
Placement	In the south	In the north
Associated Element	Fire	Water
Body Appendage	Right leg	Right leg
Element Combination	South = staves North = swords West = cups East = coins	South = cups North = coins West = staves East = swords

Overwhelming - Temperate

When you look at these two cards, as they are depicted in modern decks, you find that Temperance hasn't changed much. Strength, on the other hand, has changed quite dramatically. In pairing these two cards, we find that they speak more to selecting a proper response to a particular situation. Rather than saying that the 'strength' referred to is an inner one, what is implied in older forms of the card is an overwhelming force. This is illustrated by showing someone overpowering a lion, by use of force. Sometimes a situation calls for this "overwhelming force," sometimes it doesn't. This is in direct contradiction to what is illustrated by the Temperance card.

The Temperance card is about the use of moderation and cautiously applied actions. The old idea of tempering wine with just a little bit of water, not too little, but, not too much either, is what the card is about. The wise person knows what is necessary for any particular situation, and applying the proper response is what distinguishes the fool from the sage.

Justice and Judgement (complementary cards)

Alternate Titles		
Card's Group	Virtues	Virtues
Placement	In the west	In the east
Associated Element	Air	Earth
Body Appendage	Right leg	Right leg
Element Combination	South = swords North = staves West = coins East = cups	South = coins North = cups West = swords East = staves

Strictness - Wisdom

The pair of cards called "Justice" and "Judgement" point to different methods of dealing with the law. "Justice" is about strictly adhering to the "letter of the law," whereas "judgement" speaks to us of using wise and prudent decision-making skills. It has been said, "the letter of the law, kills the law." This means that sometimes, adhering to the strict implementation of a law can nullify the intent of writing the law in the first place. For example, the zero tolerance policies of certain schools in not having weapons on their premises is meant to protect students, but applying that rule to a student for simply drawing a gun on a piece of paper and then punishing that student with expulsion, hurts the student more than the drawing ever could have.

The policy which was intended to protect students actually hurts one instead. Good judgement has been sacrificed here to the "letter of the law" and someone's idea of what "justice" is. This is why judges, in a court of law, are often given the ability to pass judgement in a manner that does not always abide by the laws as written. This is because there are times when very special circumstances may arise that require good judgement rather literal-minded adherence to a law.

The Hanged Man and the Devil (complementary cards)

Alternate Titles	Le Pendu	Le Diable
Card's Group	Humors	Humors
Placement	In the north	In the south
Associated Element	Water	Fire
Body Appendage	Left leg	Left leg
Element Combination	South = cups North = coins West = swords East = staves	South = staves North = swords West = coins East = cups

Phlegmatic - Choleric

The Hanged Man, as the opposite of the Devil card, is the man that is hard to move. He is waiting. It takes a lot to rile this person; they have adopted a "wait-and-see" attitude. As a card associated with the water element, the Hanged Man rests, much as water rests. It is not until water is moved by an exterior force, such as wind, earth, or some other force, that water actually does something. Otherwise, it just lies there. The Hanged Man is unemotional and calm; this is in direct contradiction to the Devil card.

The Devil's element is fire. Fire is aggressive, hot, and destroys everything in its path. The Devil is hot-tempered and easy to anger. The littlest infraction, or annoyance, will set him off.

———————

The Chariot and the Hermit (complementary cards)

Alternate Titles		L'hermite
Card's Group	Humors	Humors
Placement	In the west	In the east
Associated Element	Air	Earth
Body Appendage	Left leg	Left leg
Element Combination	South = swords North = staves West = cups East = coins	South = coins North = cups West = staves East = swords

Sanguine - Melancholy

The pairing of the Chariot and Hermit cards illustrate two ways of interacting with the world at large. One is about the joy of being open and out in the public eye, while the other is closed and introverted, away from everyone.

The Chariot card is an image that refers to the sanguine humor, which is about triumph, the end of trials and a joyous finish to a great adventure. The ancient Romans had their triumphal parade, in which a returning hero was honored by being driven in a chariot before a cheering crowd of onlookers. The card represents the sun setting in the west, after successfully overcoming the trials of the day.

The Hermit, on the other hand, is about being away from the hustle and bustle of the crowd. He seeks solitude, in order to meditate and become more introspective. The Hermit's attitude is exactly the opposite of the expansive nature of the Chariot. The Hermit looks to move away from people, away from interaction with others. It is because of this lack of interaction that the Hermit can seem depressed, or melancholy, as opposed to the sanguine nature of the Chariot.

The Secret of the Hanged Man and the Hanged Man Reversed

As we have now seen, the system of the Tarot is based on a long series of dichotomies, a series of opposites that not only oppose, but, lend support to one another. Each of the elements have opposites; for example, fire to water, or air to earth. Figures depicted on the cards themselves have opposites to each other; males to females, young to old. Specific cards, in the trump section of the deck, are opposite to one another, such as the Sun and Moon, the Fool and Mage, and the Emperor and Empress. By taking this idea of "opposites," that important innovation in philosophy by the Pythagoreans, and applying it to the Hanged Man we get something very interesting.

The Hanged Man has always been said to be hiding the secret of the Tarot system. The figure of the Hanged Man traditionally is depicted as a man hanging upside down with his legs being crossed, one leg bent at the knee to cross the other leg, and the man's arms are tied behind his back; the upper body forming a downward pointing triangle, with the points of the triangle being the two elbows and head. If we were to draw this diagram over the figure of the Hanged Man we would have this:

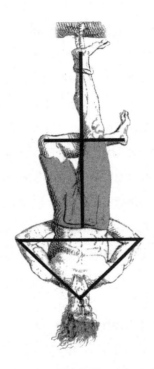

The Hanged Man with Cross and Triangle

If we were to reverse this figure, to give us an "opposite" of him, the first thing we would naturally do is turn the man right side up, so that he is in a standing posture. This was accidentally done in the printing of one of the older decks. So, the opposite of a "hanged man" is a man that is standing upright. Looking at the man's extremities to find their opposites, we uncross his legs, because "crossed" and "uncrossed" are opposite to each other, and we untie his hands, so they are free at his side, because "bound" and "free" are opposites. Now we draw another stick figure and we have this:

The Hanged Man with Pentagram Figure

Combining these two figures, we arrive at this figure:

The Hanged Man with His Opposite

We now take this figure and rotate it around a center point so that there is a figure like this in all four of the cardinal directions; east, west,

north, and south. This is the resulting diagram.
Compare it now to the figure on page 11 entitled
"Secret Layout of the Tarot:"

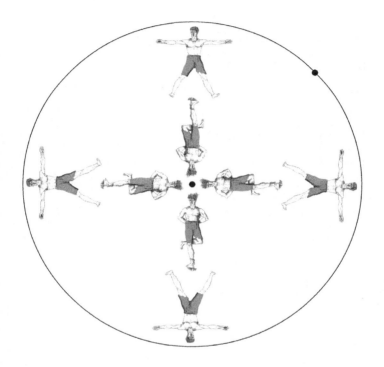

The Hanged Man Revealing the Secret Pattern

What we have in each of the cardinal
directions is an upright man that can be
represented by a pentagram, and another man,
upside down, that can be represented by an
equilateral cross and a triangle, or tetractis.

These figures revolve around the center point representing the Magician card, while the Fool card wanders the perimeter of the circle.

Now that we know that the Tarot has a structure based on a series of dichotomies and the number four, which if you will remember is what the word "tetractis" means, then it is a fairly simple task to see how the "secret pattern" is derived from that. By looking at the cards placed into the pattern, we can deduce the actual meanings of the cards by their now revealed relationships. The posture of the Hanged Man was indeed the clue left to us by those ancient masters as to the meaning of the Tarot cards.

Summation

It has always been rumored that a group, or council, of the wise had appropriated the game of cards and remodeled the deck according to their principles and teachings. We know that the earliest standardized Tarot decks appeared in Italy. From what has been described in this book, we can see that there is a strong connection between its structure and symbols to the Pythagorean school of thought. We also know that Pythagoras settled in Croton, Italy and started a school there in 530 B.C.E. The school was many things; an academy, a club, a religious organization. Eventually it became the target of fierce persecution and it closed, but not before influencing a great many people in the region.

There is quite a long time span between the close of the school and the first appearances of the Tarot. There is, however, a long line of thinkers that bridge the distance. Aristotle and Plato both make references to Pythagoreans of their time, and begin to absorb many Pythagorean ideas into their own teachings.

Neo-pythagorean thought is merged with Neo-platonism from about the time of Iamblichus (4th c. C.E.) and was very influential during the Middle Ages and Renaissance. It plays an important part in the thought of fifteenth-century Italian and German humanists. Could the Tarot have actually been the last final attempt by the Neo-Pythagoreans to preserve the teachings of Pythagoras, at least, in some small way? If it was, then, isn't the Tarot the "holy book" of the Western Tradition? We may never know for sure. I do know that the structure of the Tarot fits the Pythagorean model beautifully, and it is the Holy Book I use to understand my religious view of the world around me.

Appendices

Appendix 1: A Comparison of Assignment of Elements to Signs in Two Astrological Systems

Name of the Sign	Description	Ptolemaic Element Assigned	Seasonal Element Assigned	The Season
Aries	animal that bows its head and kicks up dirt before charging	fire	earth	spring
Taurus	animal that bows its head and kicks up dirt before charging	earth	earth	spring
Gemini	twins that are considered Gods of the earth	air	earth	spring
Cancer	The sun, at this time of year, is said to resemble a crab that walks sideways.	water	fire	summer
Leo	color and look of the male lion's head resembles the sun	fire	fire	summer

The Heretic's Tarot

Name of the Sign	Description	Ptolemaic Element Assigned	Seasonal Element Assigned	The Season
Virgo	virgin of the corn fields that are red and ready for harvest at this time of year	earth	fire	summer
Libra	the scales that weigh the heart against the weight of a feather	air	air	fall
Scorpio	Associated with three animals: serpent, scorpion, and eagle.	water	air	fall
Sagittarius	Centaur shooting and arrow from a bow, known as the "archer."	fire	air	fall
Capricorn	A Sea monster, usually depicted as goat upper body with fish lower body.	earth	water	winter

Appendix 1

Name of the Sign	Description	Ptolemaic Element Assigned	Seasonal Element Assigned	The Season
Aquarius	The water-bearer, pours water from a vessel.	air	water	winter
Pisces	Two fish.	water	water	winter

Appendix 2: Analysis of Assignment of the 24 Suit Combinations to the Trump Cards

When we take the four suits of the Tarot deck and combine them in every possible sequence, we can only make twenty-four combinations. Our problem, then, is to decide which of these combinations are attributed to each of the Trump cards and which two combinations are not assigned to any cards, being as there are only twenty-two cards in this section of the deck and not twenty-four. Converting the suits into elements, staves become fire, cups become water, swords become air and coins become earth. We will now take each place in a sequence as representing one of the four cardinal directions as follows: south, north, west, east, e.g. the sequence "fire, water, air, earth" would mean that fire is in the south, water in the north, air in the west and earth in the east, the sequence "water, fire, earth, air" on the other hand, would mean water is in the south, fire in the north, earth in the west and air in the east. Remembering that each of the quadrants are also associated with one of the four elements, and knowing that each element has a complement which is its "opposite" and diminishes it, we can say that an element is "properly placed" or "improperly placed" according to which quadrant in the sequence it falls e.g. fire in the south, which is "fire-in-fire" has its qualities strengthened and is therefore "properly placed," but water in the south is "water-in-fire," which has its qualities diminished and so is "improperly placed." There are also elements that have no effect on one another, good or bad, because the elements being paired are strengthened in one quality and diminished in the other, so the total effect is neutral e.g. "fire-in-air," fire has the qualities of "hot and dry" while air has the qualities of "hot and moist;" the quality "hot" is strengthened while the qualities "moist" and "dry" diminish one another.

The next step is to create a table, with all the combinations possible of the four elements, in an orderly and systematic fashion. I began by making four columns with the headings "south, north, west, and east" I took the sequence "fire, water, air, earth" as the proper order and placed

them into the top line of the columns. Twenty-
four combinations divides into four groups of six
combinations, so in the first column I put the
first element of each combination as six fires, six
waters, six airs, and six earths, following the
same sequence as across the top. Always
following this sequence, I created this table, as
you first saw it on page 74:

South	North	West	East	Effect
fire	water	air	earth	+ + + +
fire	water	earth	air	+ + - -
fire	air	earth	water	+ 0 - 0
fire	air	water	earth	+ 0 0 +
fire	earth	water	air	+ 0 0 -
fire	earth	air	water	+ 0 + 0
water	air	earth	fire	- 0 - 0
water	air	fire	earth	- 0 0 +
water	earth	fire	air	- 0 0 -
water	earth	air	fire	- 0 + 0
water	fire	air	earth	- - + +
water	fire	earth	air	- - - -
air	earth	fire	water	0 0 0 0
air	earth	water	fire	0 0 0 0
air	fire	water	earth	0 - 0 +
air	fire	earth	water	0 - - 0
air	water	earth	fire	0 + - 0
air	water	fire	earth	0 + 0 +

South	North	West	East	Effect
earth	fire	water	air	0 - 0 -
earth	fire	air	water	0 - + 0
earth	water	air	fire	0 + + 0
earth	water	fire	air	0 + 0 -
earth	air	fire	water	0 0 0 0
earth	air	water	fire	0 0 0 0

Next to this table, I created another that simply marked whether or not the element in the first table was "properly positioned" with a "plus" sign, "improperly positioned" with a "minus" sign, and "neutrally positioned" with a "zero." It was at this point that I noticed a pattern in the pluses, minuses and zeros. Taking the first column, under the heading "south" as the "intention" or "goal" of any particular combination and its most apparent face being in the brightest quadrant, the south, I classified each group of six as belonging to a particular element and quadrant. The pattern in the groups of six combinations in the "fire group" was, it turned out, a mirror image of the "water group" and flipping it down over the "water group" all the pluses and minuses lined up to match with their opposite, therefore, in adding up the matched pairs, every place in the combined table equaled "zero." The same was true when you flipped down the "air group" over the "earth group."

Now, there are two combinations that are "perfect." That is, one is "perfectly right" in that every element in the combination is "properly placed" and the other which is "perfectly wrong" in that every element in it is "improperly placed." These two combinations were the ones with four plus signs and four minus signs. I relate these two to the "two great forces" Empedocles spoke of as "love and strife." These two combinations I did not assign to any cards. Working with the patterns inherent in the groups, I then also removed the two combinations that relate, because of their position, to the first two combinations by being "perfectly neutral." These two combinations would be assigned to the cards "The Magician" and "The Fool." This left me with the twenty combinations needed for the rest of the Trump cards that divided up with five combinations in each quadrant. Remember that the number five equates to the pentangle and the human body with its five extremities. The head relates to the overall guiding principles of the "planets," the right hand as the controlling hand relates to the "authorities," the left hand as the uncontrollable hand to the "fates," the right leg as the strongest appendage of the body relates to the "virtues," and finally the left leg to the attitude of the body relates to the "humors."

Looking at the body, we can see that the hands and legs each have an opposite partner, whereas the head is alone and balanced between the left and right sides. Applying this to the five remaining combinations in each group, we see that there are four that "mirror" one another, just as the groups had previously, but has only one combination that is "balanced" and not mirrored within the group. Because of this, I assigned each of these "balanced combinations" to the planet cards as follows:

Fire Group	The Sun card	+ + - -
Water Group	The Moon card	- - + +
Air Group	The Star card	0 0 0 0
Earth Group	The World card	0 0 0 0

Looking back across at the original combinations of elements, I could then assign a particular combination, from the twenty-four possible, to each of these cards. This was the result:

	South	North	West	East
The Sun	Fire	Water	Earth	Air
The Moon	Water	Fire	Air	Earth
The Star	Air	Earth	Water	Fire
The World	Earth	Air	Fire	Water

The "Planetary" group of trump cards.

Notice how the The Sun card's elemental combination is a complement of the The Moon card's, and the same is true for The Star and World cards. In other words, if I change all of the elements in any particular combination to their complementary element, then I get the combination that would be assigned to a complementary card as well.

Now that I had assigned combinations to each of the "planetary" cards, what remained was four combinations in each of the four groups to assign to the remaining appendages of hands and feet, and their cards. I looked first at the fire group. The five cards of this group are: Sun, Emperor, Lightning Struck Tower, Strength and the Devil. The Sun card had already been assigned to a combination, so it was time to assign the next four cards in the group. I noticed, in the combinations of "fire," that there were pluses all the way down the first column, so I eliminated this column from consideration, since it could not possibly distinguish one of the cards in the group from another, they being all the same. Looking at the zeros, pluses and minuses in the combinations, I noticed that they were all zeros, except for one plus and one minus in each combination. This was the distinguishing factor in each combination.

After trying many different ways of ways of attributing the combinations and coming up with no clear distinctions between them, I came upon this method: each group has its "own impulse," that is, a way to evaluate a strongly placed element within the structure of the group. Each group has a combination that is completely one "set of signs," whether pluses, minuses or zeros. That combination, that is "all one sign," would define for that any particular group what position is strengthened by its position.

In one of the "fire" combinations, there was a plus in the "earth" column. Pluses in this group means that the element is well-placed there, so it is enhanced or strengthened. Earth relates directly to the right leg and the virtues. The virtue card for "fire" was "Strength," so I assigned this card to that combination. Another plus was in the "air" column. Air relates to the left hand and the fates, so I assigned this combination to the "Lightning Struck Tower" card. Looking at these two combinations as "opposites," right foot being lower right, while the left hand is upper left, we then notice that there two other opposites in the fire group, the two minus signs. These two should be assigned to the final two cards of the fire group, which are the Emperor and Devil cards; they will be assigned to the left leg and right hand. But the question remains, "which combination, to which appendage?"

Here is where I made a comparison between the two signs in the same column. If a plus in the column representing the right leg meant the element placed there was "strong," then a minus must mean it is weak there and therefore "strong" in its "opposite." Since there is a possibility for two opposites, right leg to left hand, or, right leg to right hand, I simply chose the one that was not already allocated a card. So the combination with a minus sign in earth related to a positive aspect for the right hand, and therefore that combination was assigned to the Emperor card. This reasoning also worked for the final combination, and I assigned it to the Devil card. Here are the combination assignments for the "fire group:"

	South	North	West	East
The Sun	Fire	Water	Earth	Air
The Emperor	Fire	Earth	Water	Air

	South	North	West	East
The Tower	Fire	Earth	Air	Water
The Devil	Fire	Air	Earth	Water
Strength	Fire	Air	Water	Earth

The "fire" group of trump cards.

Moving on the the next grouping, the "water group," the plus and minus signs are exactly opposite of those in the "fire group," so we take as "strengthened" those placements that have a minus sign in them and following the same logic as in the previous group. What we arrive at is the following assignment of combinations:

	South	North	West	East
The Moon	Water	Fire	Air	Earth
The Empress	Water	Air	Fire	Earth
The Lovers	Water	Air	Earth	Fire
Hanged Man	Water	Earth	Air	Fire

	South	North	West	East
Temperance	Water	Earth	Fire	Air

The "water" group of trump cards.

Comparing the elements in these two groups, you can see that when you change each element in a particular combination to its opposite, e.g. fire to water, earth to air, water to fire and air to earth, then the resulting combination is assigned to a card which is "opposite" to the card of the original combination. In some cases the pair of opposite cards is fairly plain to understand; however, in others it reveals a not-so-apparent meaning to the cards. For example, it is easy to see the Moon as the opposite card of the Sun, but applying the same method pairs up some interesting cards, like the Devil with the Hanged Man. This pairing points out the qualities of the Devil as quick to anger (choleric) in contrast with the Hanged Man's qualities of stoic patience (phlegmatic).

Next, I tackled the "air and earth groups." If I were to follow the same logic as in the two previous groups, then the strengthened elements within the group's structure would have to be marked with zeros, as both groups had as their ruling influence two lines of zeros. This presented a problem, because in the "fire and water groups" there were pluses and minuses to distinguish between "weakened" and "strengthened" elements. I noticed the pattern in the two prior groups of pluses and minuses were now being replaced by zeros. I remembered something from a math class, long ago. In using "imaginary numbers" there could be such a thing as a "positive zero" or "negative zero." The only way to make any distinction between the elements in these two groups would be to figure out which zeros were "positive zeros" and which were "negative zeros" and use that to determine the strengths and weaknesses of the elements here.

I next noticed that the patterns of pluses and minuses in the fire and water groups were now being followed by the zeros in the air and earth groups. Keeping the patterns intact, I overlaid the pluses and minuses from the fire and water groups onto the air and earth groups and discovered that the patterns matched perfectly. The fire group's pattern matched the air group's and water group's matched the earth group's. This gave me the positive and negative zeros I needed. Now it was simply a matter of following the same logic as before, according to the group's pattern, fire to air and water to earth and I assigned the following cards to the combinations in the air and earth groups.

	South	North	West	East
The Star	Air	Earth	Water	Fire
The Priestess	Air	Water	Earth	Fire
Death	Air	Water	Fire	Earth
The Chariot	Air	Fire	Water	Earth
Justice	Air	Fire	Earth	Water

The "Air" group of trump cards.

	South	North	West	East
The World	Earth	Air	Fire	Water
The Priest	Earth	Fire	Air	Water
The Wheel	Earth	Fire	Water	Air
The Hermit	Earth	Water	Fire	Air
Judgement	Earth	Water	Air	Fire

The "Earth" group of trump cards.

Now twenty of the twenty-two Trump cards have been assigned to a combination. The final two cards needing a combination are the Fool and Magician cards. Remember there are twenty-four combinations, and we tossed the two that were "perfectly placed" and "perfectly misplaced." That leaves these two combinations to use for the final two cards.

South	North	West	East
Earth	Air	Water	Fire

South	North	West	East
Air	Earth	Fire	Water

In assigning these two combinations, we go back to something we said right at the beginning of the analysis, "Taking the first column, under the heading 'south' as the 'intention' or 'goal' of any particular combination and its most apparent face..." we can simply think about what a Fool and Magician are in their traditional roles. One combination has "earth" as its focus, and the other has "air." Earth is tangible and easy to grasp, it has to do with the superficial "look" of things, while "air" is fluid and unseen, it has to do with the spirit and the mind, things that are beneath the surface. Now think about the cards. The Fool is ignorant, naive, unfocused, and usually depicted as unaware he is about to step off a cliff. A Magician, on the other hand, is so aware and skilled that not only does he know what he is doing, he knows how it will lead you to think what he wishes you to think. The Magician controls his tools and your thoughts so well that he is able to create illusions that make you think you see something that should not be. Simply put, the world of the Fool is the material world, earth, and the world of the Magician is the world of the unseen, air. So, I assign the final two combinations like this:

	South	North	West	East
The Fool	Earth	Air	Water	Fire
The Magicia	Air	Earth	Fire	Water

The "Soul" group of trump cards.

Appendix 3: Freemasonry's Influence on Mystical Organizations

(Note: the only difference between Grand Lodge Masonry and Co-Masonry is that the latter admits men and women to its ranks, while the former only men.)

Freemasons founded the following mystical organizations:

1. Bavarian Illuminati
2. Lucis Trust
3. Theosophical Society
4. Ordo Templi Orientis
5. Hermetic Order of the Golden Dawn
6. Wiccan Religion
7. Stella Matutina
8. Astrum Argenteum
9. AMORC

Influential Freemasons:

Bailey, Alice A. (1880-1949). Co-Mason and co-founder of the Lucis Trust.

Bailey, Foster. Co-Mason and co-founder of the Lucis Trust.

Besant, Annie. Co-Mason and leader of the Theosophical Society.

Mabel Besant-Scott. Leader of Co-Masonry in Britain, after her mother's death and was Gerald Gardner's neighbor in Highcliffe, near Christchurch, on the edge of the New Forest. She was also a leading member of the Rosicrucian Fellowship of Crotona.

Blavatsky, Helena Petrovena (1831-1891). Co-Mason and wrote Isis Unveiled and The Secret Doctrine in the latter part of the 19th century. She also founded the Theosophical Society.

Cagliostro, Count (1743-1795). An Italian adventurer and self-styled magician who became a glamorous figure in the royal courts of Europe, where he reputedly excelled in various occult arts, such as psychic healing, alchemy and scrying. His real name was Giuseppe Balsamo and he came from a poor family in Palermo, Sicily. At the age of 23, he went to Malta and was initiated into the Order of the Knights of Malta where he studied alchemy, the Kabbala and other occult secrets. Later, in London, he joined the Freemasons, and subsequently spent his life roaming the royal courts in Europe performing various occult arts and peddling magic potions and an 'elixir of immortal life' with the aid of his wife, Lorenza Feliciani.[25]

Casanova, Giovanni Giacomo (1725-1798). Aside from living a now-famous romantic life, he was also a Freemason and occultist/ esotericist.

Crowley, Aleister (1875-1947). After growing up in a Plymouth Brethren home, he rejected Christianity to become the leading English occultist of the twentieth century, and a Freemason.

Crowther, Arnold (1909-1974). Freemason, English Witch, a skilled stage magician, and married to Patricia C. Crowther. Crowther was born on October 7, 1909, in Chestham, Kent, one of a pair of fraternal twins. Crowther authored, in collaboration with Patricia, two books,

---

[25] *www.occultopedia.com/c/cagliostro.htm*

numerous magazine articles, and a radio series on Witchcraft.[26]

Encausse, Dr. Gerard (Papus) (1865-1916). He organized what was announced as an "International Masonic Conference" in Paris on June 24, 1908, and at this conference, he received a patent from Theodor Reuss to establish a "Supreme Grand Council General of the Unified Rites of Antient and Primitive Masonry for the Grand Orient of France and its Dependencies at Paris." It was probably on the same occasion that Reuss conferred upon Papus the X° of O.T.O. for France, and Papus, in turn, assisted Reuss in the formation of the O.T.O. Gnostic Catholic Church as a child of l'Église Gnostic de France. When John Yarker died in 1913, Papus was elected as his successor to the office of Grand Hierophant (international head) of the Antient and Primitive Rites of Memphis and Mizraim.[27]

---

26 http://www.themystica.com/mystica/articles/c/crowther_arnold.html

27 http://www.thelemapedia.org/index.php/Gerard_Encausse

Gardner, Gerald Brousseau (1884-1964). English Freemason, occultist and creator of modern witchcraft, or "Wicca." He was a sickly child and received very little formal education. In 1900, he moved to Sri Lanka where he worked on a plantation and later became a civil servant. He traveled widely in the East, absorbing local cultures and folk beliefs. Retiring to England in 1938, he joined a Theosophical group led by the daughter of Annie Besant, through whom he met Dorothy Clutterbuck, who claimed to be a witch and initiated him into "the Craft." In 1949, under the assumed name "Scire," he published a novel High Magic's Aid where he outlined many of his ideas about magical ritual. Following the repeal of England's Witchcraft Laws in 1951, he published Witchcraft Today (1954) and numerous other books. In 1963, Gardner initiated Raymond and Rosemary Buckland who spread his creed to North America.[28]

Gebelin, Antoine Court de (1725-1784). French linguist, cleric, occultist, Freemason, member of

---

28 http://religion.enacademic.com/744/GARDNER,_Gerald_Brousseau

the Lodge of the Philalethes, and author of the nine volume work Le Monde Primitif.

Hall, Manly P. (1901-1990). Rosicrucian adept and author of popular Freemasonry manuals. In 1990, Mr. Hall was recognized as an honorary 33° Mason (the highest rank possible in the Scottish Rite).

Jennings, Hargrave (1817-1890). Was a British Freemason and amateur student of comparative religion. In several voluminous works, he argued that the origin of all religion is to be sought in phallic worship of the Sun and fire.

Leadbetter, C. W. Co-Mason and Theosophist, mentor of Krishnamurti, and prelate in the Liberal Catholic Church.

Levi, Eliphas (1810-1875). The pseudonym of Alphonse Louis Constant, a French occultist who was largely responsible for the revival of interest in magic in the 19th century. Eliphas Levi became a Freemason, initiated at the Lodge Rose du Parfait Silence. Levi studied magic and believed in it but was more of a commentator than and adept, though he did claim to practice necromancy on several occasions. His first and most important book, The Dogma and Ritual of High Magic, was published in 1861. He followed that with A History of Magic, Transcendental Magic, The Key of Great Mysteries and other occult books. Levi's magic was adopted by the Hermetic Order of the Golden Dawn, founded in London in 1888.

Lewis, Harvey Spencer (1883-1939). Freemason and famous Rosicrucian mystic, was the founder and the first Imperator of AMORC, from 1915 until 1939.

Mathers, S. L. MacGregor. Freemason and co-founder of the Golden Dawn.

McKenzie, Kenneth R. H. Member of the Golden Dawn and author of a Masonic Encyclopedia.

Pickingill, George (1816-1909). Freemason, witch and sorcerer in England and leader of the "Pickingill covens."

Pike, Albert (1809-1891). Author of "Morals and Dogma" the Masonic book of doctrine. Borrowed extensively from the books of Eliphas Levi for material for his own books.

Reuss, Dr. Theodore (1855-1923). Freemason and one-time head of the society Ordo Templi Orientis.

Sanders, Alexander (1929-1988). Freemason and self-styled "King of the Witches" based in London, England, and one of the most influential leaders of Wicca after Gardner.

St-Germain, Count de. Although no one knew when the Count de St. Germain was born, his life from 1710 to 1822 is a matter of history. Intimate and counselor of Kings and Princes, nemesis of deceptive ministers, Rosicrucian, Freemason, accredited Messenger of the Masters of Wisdom; worked in Europe for more than a century, faithfully performing the difficult task which had been entrusted to him.

Waite, Arthur Edward (1857-1942). He was an English occultist, Freemason, and member of "The Hermetic Order of the Golden Dawn" which he joined in 1891 (and apparently again in 1896 after quitting them) ...and it was he that had their name changed in 1903 to "The Holy Order of the Golden Dawn." He was more into the mysticism side of the occult and later with the famous William Butler Yeats would found a new order, "The Stella Matutina."

Weishaupt, Adam (1748-1830). A Freemason, he was initiated into a Lodge of Strict Observance, Lodge Theodore of Good Council, at Munich in 1777; founder of the Bavarian Illuminati.

Westcott, Dr. Wynn (1848-1925). Freemason and founding member of the occult Order of the Golden Dawn; the most influential magical society of the 19th and early 20th century.

Woodman, Dr. William Robert (1828–1891). Freemason and co-founder of the Hermetic Order of the Golden Dawn.

Bibliography

Aveni, Anthony F. Conversing with the Planets: How Science and Myth Invented the Cosmos. Times Books, 1992.

Barnes, Harry Elmer. An Intellectual and Cultural History of the Western World, Vol. One: From Earliest Times through the Middle Ages. Dover Publications, Inc., 1965.

Butler, Bill. Dictionary of the Tarot. Schocken Books, New York, 1975.

Campbell, Joseph, and Richard Roberts. Tarot Revelations. 3rd ed. Vernal Equinox Press, 1987.

Cirlot, Juan Eduardo. A Dictionary of Symbols. 2nd ed. Philosophical Library, 1971.

Clifton, Chas S. Gnosis Magazine. Article: The Unexamined Tarot. Issue #18, page 44.

Decker, Ronald, Thierry Depaulis, and Michael Dummett. A Wicked Pack of Cards: The Origins of the Occult Tarot. Palgrave Macmillan, 1996.

Dummett, Michael. The Visconti-Sforza Tarot Cards. George Braziller, 1986.

Dunne, Michael. Magistri Petri de Ybernia. Expositio et quaestiones in Aristotelis Librum de longitudine et brevitate vitae. Peeters Publishers. 1993.

Gleadow, Rupert. The Origin of the Zodiac. Atheneum, 1969.

Guthrie, Kenneth S. The Pythagorean Sourcebook and Library. Phanes Press, Grand Rapids, Michigan, USA 1987.

Jung, Carl G. Alchemical Studies: Translated by R. F. C. Hull. Princeton University Press, 1983.

Jung, Carl G. Man and His Symbols. Dell Publishing Co., Inc. 1968.

Kaplan, Stuart R., and Jean Huets. The Encyclopedia Of Tarot, Vol. 1. U.S. Games Systems, 1977.

Kaplan, Stuart R. Tarot Classic Cards. U.S. Games Systems, 1974.

Knight, Gareth. The Treasure House of Images. Destiny Books, Rochester, Vermont, 1986.

Levi, Eliphas. Transcendental Magic. Samuel Weiser, 1979.

Lightfoot, Jewel P. Lightfoot's manual of the lodge; or, Monitorial instructions in the three degrees of symbolic masonry: As exemplified in the Grand jurisdiction of Texas, ... and allegories of ancient craft masonry. Masonic Home & School, Dept. of Printing, 1936.

Mackey, Albert. Mackey's Revised Encyclopedia of Freemasonry. The Masonic history company, 1946.

Newton, Joseph Fort. The Builders: A Story and Study of Masonry. Plain Label Books, 1924.

Pike, Albert. Morals and Dogma of the Ancient and Accepted Scottish Rite of Freemasonry Prepared for the Supreme Council of the Thirty-third Degree, for the Southern Jurisdiction of the United States, and Published By Its Authority. Charleston Southern Jurisdiction, 1919.

Jones, Prudence and Pennick, Nigel. A History of Pagan Europe. Routledge, London and New York, 1995.

Wright, M. R. Cosmology in Antiquity. Routledge, 1965.

Bibliography

Made in the USA
Las Vegas, NV
12 April 2021

21253813R00144